Prospects on Cooperative Entrepreneurship Development System in India

Dr.S. Thangaraju

Published by

Prospects on Cooperative Entrepreneurship Development System in India

ISBN 978-93-86176-06-6

Author

Dr.S. Thangaraju

Bonfring
309, 2nd Floor, 5th Street Extension, Gandhipuram,
Coimbatore-641 012.
Tamilnadu, India.
E-mail: info@bonfring.org | Website: www.bonfring.org
Phone: 0422-3928700

Preface

Cooperative sector has offered self-employment opportunities that can contribute to small scale industries and Agricultural Development in India. After economic reform, those systems had been changed drastically. As a result majority of the cooperative organizations were partially undertaken by the Government. Because of equal share allocation by private sector, they can role play for entire corner of Industrial, Service and Agricultural sector. The support system is encouraging them in order to development sector works which comes under Public Private Partnership. The effects of such changes for economic and social pattern of people, they are unable to maintained self sustained and self realization by economic viability through cooperative sector. Therefore, we need a separate system for Entrepreneurs Development Programmes through pure cooperative policy and principles. There is no involvement and intervention by Government decisions or politician's role. Hence, this book describes about the nature and realistic approach on emerge and developed an Entrepreneurship System through Cooperatives. Example, if Sugar Cooperatives have huge or surplus funds, they may have support to other processing Cooperatives for mutual support for long run approach without financial restrictions. Moreover, this book is very useful to the policy makers and researchers who are going to pursue in the Areas of New Dimensions of Agriculture or Industrial sector Action Research.

CHAPTER-I

Introduction

By and large, the observation made by Martin Luther King has been commonly accepted and even can be applied in today's fast changing world accompanied by the liberalization of world economy. He said "**the ultimate measure of a man is not where he stands in moments of comfort and convenience, but where he stands, at times of challenge and controversy**". The emerging entrepreneurs and even those operating under cooperative umbrella, are exclusively facing many types of challenges, threads and problems (inconveniences) in coping up with the business and commercial competitive environment. In the recent times, new outlook, posterity, wealth creation and long-term prosperity are only possible when young entrepreneurs took up the issue of self-employment into their hands through enterprises. The sources of gainful employment scenario in the current competitive environment are deteriorating day in and day out. In fact, unemployment scenario and sometimes nil income are the order of the day in both rural and urban areas.

The pillars of employment creations are unduly neglected by the economic planners and administrators. It shows the highest level of hard times ahead of every human being in this world, where scarce to very scarce employment opportunities would prevail. Many a time, gainful employment opportunities and income generating ventures are becoming dim, grim and even becoming very limited. To that extent, many educated and self-supportive men and women undertake self-employment, developmental activities to rescue themselves from serious unemployment problems. Though, much significance has been given to promote viable and sustainable development programs in entrepreneurship schemes, suitable and appropriate strategies and methods have not been effectively and efficiently formulated and implemented. A full-fledge involvement of all the Central & State Planning Commissions and Committees of the government and even more importantly by the cooperative sector itself have given scanty recognition to cooperative entrepreneurship. Therefore, there is an urgent need for developing new democratic set up of cooperative entrepreneurship system under the modem cooperative fold to cater to the urgent needs of the new emerging entrepreneurs.

Furthermore, the era of economic liberalization and globalization has brought forth more bright chances, for the development and growth of many small and medium scale industries/organizations which can be managed and administered through cooperative approach. More and frequent financial assistance are given by various, commercial, private and foreign banking organizations and their subsidiaries for developing entrepreneurs, but less importance is given to develop these enterprises through cooperative entrepreneurship programmes/systems. Fund mobilization is no more a hindrance in forming and evolving viable cooperative enterprises by various entrepreneurs, rather leadership qualities, skills, attitude, knowledge, competencies, capacity etc. It is noteworthy for instance that, various banking and non-banking financial institutions are supplying financial assistance through various schemes at different interest rates for the entrepreneurs to exploit the emerging business opportunities. Thus, cooperative entrepreneurs approach can become the sine-qua-non developing new entrepreneurship system in the future or even in the new millennium. Moreover, the New Generation Cooperative Entrepreneurship (NGCE) Systems/Programmes should take advantage of the new technology, communication and information system. They must learn how to use the latest/modern ways of managing commercial organizations and business activities. They can even access funds from international organizations such as Asian Development Bank (ADB), Industrial Development Banks, Industrial & commercial banks, long-term credit banks, HSBC etc.

Beneficiary

Co-operatives are run for the benefit of their members; they achieve this benefit in a number of ways. First, the co-operative should meet a commonly-defined need. For example, this could be the need for employment amongst a group of graduates; a need for broadband services in a remote community; or the need for social care services in a town/city. Second, the co-operative should generate a range of economic, social and psychological benefits; these could be secure employment, a decent wage, a share of any surplus generated, democratic control over your working life, or addressing a social/community issue. Third, the co-operative should distribute some of the surplus generated amongst its members. A note of caution on the distribution of surplus: while the thought of a large share of the surplus might appeal in the short-term, you will probably not be in business for very long if 100 per cent of the surplus is given to the members.

Most co-operatives set a limit on how much can be distributed to members (usually 50-70 per cent) and the rest is retained in the business as reserves. Some co-operatives choose to commit a certain percentage of profit to social and/or community goals as well, fulfilling the seventh co-operative principle.

Values and Principles

Co-operatives can take many forms but attempts have been made to produce a common definition and set of values and principles to unite co-operatives globally. The International Co-operative Alliance (ICA), a global federation of co-operatives, defines a co-operative as: 'an autonomous association of persons united voluntarily to meet their common economic, social, and cultural needs and aspirations through a jointly-owned and democratically-controlled enterprise.'

To supplement this definition, a set of values and principles was also produced, in keeping with ideas that drove the original founders of the co-operative movement in the nineteenth century. The values of equity, equality, solidarity, democracy, self-help, and self-responsibility are central to the purpose of a co-operative and these values are put into practice through seven principles:

1. Voluntary and Open Membership

Co-operatives are voluntary organizations, open to all persons able to use their services and willing to accept the responsibilities of membership, without gender, social, racial, political or religious discrimination.

2. Democratic Member Control

Co-operatives are democratic organizations controlled by their members, who actively participate in setting their policies and making decisions. Men and women serving as elected representatives are accountable to the membership. In primary co-operatives members have equal voting rights (one member, one vote), and co-operatives at other levels are also organized in a democratic manner.

3. Member Economic Participation

Members contribute equitably to, and democratically control, the capital of their co operative. At least part of that capital is usually the common property of the co-operative. Members usually receive limited compensation, if any, on capital subscribed as a condition of membership. Members allocate surpluses for any of the following purposes: developing their co-operative, possibly by setting up reserves, part of which at least would be indivisible; benefiting members in proportion to their transactions with the co-operative; and supporting other activities approved by the membership.

4. Autonomy and Independence

Co-operatives are autonomous, self-help organizations controlled by their members. If they enter into agreements with other organizations, including governments, or raise capital from external sources, they do so on terms that ensure democratic control by their members and maintain their co-operative autonomy.

5. Education, Training and Information

Co-operatives provide education and training for their members, elected representatives, managers and employees so they can contribute effectively to the development of their co-operatives. They inform the general public–particularly young people and opinion leaders about the nature and benefits of co-operation.

6. Co-operation among Co-operatives

Co-operatives serve their members most effectively and strengthen the cooperative movement by working together through local, regional, national and international structures.

7. Concern for Community

Co-operatives work for the sustainable development of their communities through policies approved by their members. Noted that the co-operative values and principles are descriptive of what a co-operative should be rather than prescriptive. So long as your business is member-owned, democratically controlled and distributes some of its economic benefits to members, it will generally be accepted as a co-operative. It means, the values and principles provide a powerful platform for conducting business in an economically and socially successful manner.

The Co-operative Scenario in Transition Countries

As a result of the collapse of centrally-planned economies, the next challenge was to re-establish both a co-operative identity and a new co-operative system. In the first phase of transition, governments opposed co-operatives, considering them part of the "inherited" social and economic structure. Their transformation into capitalistic companies was preferred12 to the recognition of the potential of co-operatives in an emerging civil society-the creation of civil communities and economic coordination of the citizens. At the beginning of the transition, the literature on economic reform was in general critical of the potential role of employee ownership in enterprise restructuring: it was expected to pro-mote large wage increases and inflationary pressures, a deterioration in economic performance, considerable delays in restructuring, labour hoarding, and a low propensity to carry out necessary investments. This privatization form was rarely proposed in policy documents and its negative effects were systematically presented, while its potential advantages were completely ignored (Vaughan White-head, 1998). As compared with the alternative of external ownership of joint stock companies, employee-owned firms are instead more likely to be characterized by a focused, tightly-knit ownership group with a strong stake in the enterprise performance. In such firms, the security and stability of the enterprise and its work will weigh more heavily in decision making. Accordingly, insider ownership and insider control is more conducive to enterprise stability and long term relationships and thus may contribute to better economic performance (Jones, Mygind, 2000).

With the decline of communist regimes, co-operatives had to reorient their business strategy and develop entrepreneurial skills. The transition towards a market-oriented economic system took various forms:

- Restitution of property to former owners (Czech Republic, former German Democratic Republic);
- Privatization by means of negotiable coupons, distributed to members, employees and former owners and sold to interested parties (Hungary, Russian Federation, Baltic States);
- Dissolution and liquidation (Todev, Brazda, Schediwy, 1993)13. Consequently, while some countries decided to dissolve all politicised unions and federations, others developed a sort of "planned transition", also through employee ownership.

Nevertheless, recent developments show that a total disintegration of federal structures has usually led to a change of co-operatives into other legal forms and, thus, to a total de-co-operatization (Brazda, Todev, 1993).

However, the efforts to "depoliticise" co-operative unions, federations and apex organizations proved to be difficult. Not only was there a lack of leaders with experience of autonomous, market-oriented co-operatives but the primary co-operatives were weak and disoriented through the transition process.

The International Labor Organization (ILO) points out two major obstacles to the development of the co-operative sector in former socialist countries:

First of all, a major obstacle to the establishment of new service co-operatives of farmers, traders, craftsmen and members of liberal professions was that during the first years of the new regime, there were not enough private farms, businesses and individual entrepreneurs to constitute a membership, even after decades of collectivization.

- Another obstacle was the lack of an adequate legislative framework regarding ownership of land, property rights and access to financial services. In addition, there was no effective administrative machinery to put the new legislation into effect. Although the economy was liberalized at high speed, reforms of government structures at national, regional and local levels lagged behind so that these structures remained largely unchanged (ILO, 2001, p. 19-23);
- An additional problem is created by the introduction of market re-forms while allowing socialist structures and thought processes to still exist throughout the public administration, and of introducing private property of means of production without corresponding property rights and chances for the private owners to exercise their rights.

It has become clear that privatization and transformation not only re-quire legal and economic restructuring, but also create socio-psychological problems for those involved at all levels, making it more difficult to find solutions. This means that "the abolition of ideological influences upon the economy coupled with the admission of a variety of forms in the economy are mandatory requirements for the development of autonomous co-operatives" (Münkner, 1998). Prejudice towards the co-operative form in fact prevents this organizational form from developing in an environment characterized by an unregulated emergence of other types of organizations formally belonging to the third sector (voluntary organizations, self-help organizations, community organizations, religious organizations), regardless of the lack of legal provisions for organizational forms.

At present, the co-operative development paths as evident in the former communist countries are above all connected to the existence of adequate legislative frameworks that focus ownership of land, property rights and access to financial services, and the involvement of the co-operative movements in the legislative process.

However, while the traditional co-operative sectors are in decline, newly established co-operatives, such as credit unions (which were wiped out under the planned system), housing co-operatives and agricultural co-operatives are increasingly being looked upon as effective social tools, capable of fighting against social exclusion and the increasing unemployment concern that resulted from the dismantling of the former industrial structure.

As many state enterprises have been closed down, new types of activities have been set up within the consumer co-operatives, such as shoe re-pairs, clothes sewing, photo studios, pharmacies in rural areas. Yet private firms have not replaced state enterprises, co-operatives, especially consumer co-operatives, might have a gap to fill (Sätre Ahlander, 2000).

In particular, while co-operatives are returning to their original roots, they have an important role to play in sustaining both social and economic development. And notwithstanding the apparent "co-operative vacuum", in the long term co-operatives will surely become indispensable institutions of agricultural, rural and social development. With respect to agriculture, as a result of both the increasing competition within the global market and the lessening of support given by governments, farmers will need to look for new solutions.

In this respect, agricultural co-operatives will have an important role to play in these issues (Pattison, 2000). Co-operative action could be effective in promoting the consolidated tenure of highly fragmented landed properties, by establishing "land renting" co-operatives. Similarly, a number of services could be supplied through co-operatives. The dismantling of the former system created indeed a hiatus of service providers not replaced at present by either private or the public sectors. Transition countries could learn from the experience of European countries. This applies to social services (health, elderly and child-care, etc.) (Copac, 1999),which could be successfully supplied through co-operatives. What emerges is the potential of co-operatives as community organizations, which are increasingly showing a positive impact on both economic development and the process of democratization. In particular, such kind of co-operatives should be considered as significant tools for social change.

As social tools, co-operatives can be used to foster social cohesion, which is threatened by a sharp rise in poverty, growing unemployment rates and high levels of inequalities, resulting in a sharp social stratification of the population. alongside the long-established co-operative enterprises (agricultural supply and marketing societies, credit societies, consumer, etc.), growing over the last decades into large-scale enterprises, behaving almost like investor-owned companies and going through a number of crises resulting in either their disappearance or reduction, new co-operative fields of development are increasingly emerging (and re-emerging) in both Western and Eastern countries.

In particular, new co-operatives which are naturally addressed to the local community stand out, as they offer life-quality enhancing benefits that can both serve disadvantaged people and the community at large. The interest on co-operative evolution towards a socially oriented model arises from its strong connection with the evolution of traditional welfare models towards a "welfare community" model. However, this trend determined a number of changes of the organisational and corporate models, partly assimilated by the law.

Moreover, this is particularly interesting and relevant for "transition countries" for two different reasons: developing a private economy and co-operative system and creating a new welfare system. On the one hand, the need for traditional co-operatives is becoming apparent. On the other, the lack of public expenditure-due to cuts in budgets, following the abandon of the planned economic system-addressed to the production of personal and social services, calls for new alternative solutions, among which stands out the bottom-up supply of community care services through the means of self-help. In this respect, the co-operative model may represent an effective means both for accelerating the transition and contributing to reduce a number of problems, like low labour demand and poverty, and for providing new solutions to cope with growing social problems.

Co-operative Movement and Contemporary Communities

The *Statement of Co-operative Identity* was a reaction to four major contemporary trends: the disintegration of the centrally planned economies of Central and Eastern Europe; the unclear roles of co-ops in many Southern countries; the overpowering dominance of market ideologies and classical liberal thought; and increased global integration through technology - the advent of what Marshall McLuhan had called *the global village.* The search for this statement unknowingly began with Alexander Laid-law's report (1980) on *Co-operatives in the Year 2000*, prepared for the Moscow Congress of 1980. Laidlaw was a good choice for that task: he had travelled widely for someone of his generation and he knew about co-ops in many parts of the world. He was the protégé of Moses Coady, the principal founder of the Antigonish movement at St. Francis Xavier University and Canada's most profound co-operative theorist in the mid-twentieth century. Coady, in fact, was the person who popularized the term "Big Picture" in his speeches and writings (Walton, 2001; Laidlaw, 1971).

Laidlaw identified several challenges confronting co-ops: declining member commitment; weakening democratic participation; neglect of education; poor communication systems; uncertain roles for elected leaders; how they might better serve the poor; uneven employment practices; and sectoral disunity. All these problems involved the ways in which co-operatives were situated in their societies, how they encouraged member involvement, and how they responded to communities.

Laidlaw anticipated four major opportunities, all of them as much social as economic: feeding a hungry world; providing productive labour; contributing to a conserver society, and building co-operative communities.

In 1984 at the Hamburg Congress Michael Trunov of the then Soviet Union prepared another paper that considered the social roles of co-operatives. He argued that the international movement needed to take more responsibility for building global peace, encouraging new co-op development, ensuring greater food security, and counteracting environmental degradation. He ran into opposition from those who resisted the idea that the co-op movement should be "used" (as some interpreted his approach), but many were attracted to the idea that co-op should address the major issues of the time.

Lars Marcus (1988), the President of the ICA in 1988, built on these reports and extrapolated from his own experiences to challenge the international movement to reconsider its basic values and rethink its fundamental commitments. Marcus spoke from his efforts to expand the ICA's work beyond its North Atlantic and particularly its European base. He was also committed to expanding the ICA's base beyond its traditional consumer co-operative core to include more genuinely all kinds of co-operative enterprise. That process had begun in the 1950s through the work of several leaders, many of them, like Nils Thedin (1988), also from Scandinavia. It was demonstrated in the opening of the India Office in 1960 and the Moshe office in 1968. Marcus and the ICA Director, Bruce Thordarson, continued the process as they oversaw the opening of an office in Central America, the regionalization of the ICA governance/managerial structure, and the beginnings of ICA international co-operative development projects.

These were big changes for the ICA, shaking old patterns of association and posing significant managerial problems, as Marcus's paper at the 1988 Stockholm Congress and subsequent events indicate. It was one thing, in the *cliché* of the times, to think globally and act locally; it was another to actually do it. The challenges, moreover, were greater than Laidlaw had anticipated and they formed a menacing background as the discussions developed. Older co-ops, in particular, were changing dramatically as they were buffeted by what became popularly called globalization in the 1990s: the intensification of international markets; the creation of large economic blocks, like the European Common Market and the North America Free Trade Area; the rapid transformation of communications systems; the re-engineering of firms into flatter management systems; the increased mobility of capital; the "outsourcing" of labour; the declining roles of the state and entitlements; and the emphasis on economics over social policy. For many co-operators caught up in these issue, it could be a bewildering and unwelcome diversion from essential duties. For others, though, particularly outside of the North Atlantic, it was a vital exercise, one to be engaged with considerable enthusiasm.

The next step in the process was an international dialogue on co-operative values, led by Sven Akë Böök of Sweden (1992). Lasting from 1988 to 1992, it culminated in the book *Co-operative Values in a Changing World,* written by Böök after extensive research and numerous meetings around the world. In it, he tried to reflect the wide, rich and diverse range of views he had found. The result is a volume that is not "an easy read," its central arguments tending to be circular in ways more appreciated in non-Western intellectual traditions. It does not always follow the linear logic that has dominated Western thought since the eighteenth century, though it might be argued that it also reflects co-operative intellectual traditions rather well; traditions that are much more preoccupied with understanding ambiguities and shaping consensus than in finding irrefutable and permanent truth.

Böök's study heightened discussions about community values and social obligations. He focused primarily on the movement and its institutions as he sought to make a coherent whole out of the enormously rich experiences and value systems he found within the international movement. He produced an essentially inward-looking document, recognizing the importance of new types of co-ops, particularly social co-operatives; the roles of co-ops in emancipating people from poverty and oppression; and the need for a new, broad and empowering vision.

Thus even before Manchester, there was a tendency within the international movement to reconsider the relationship between "community" and co-operatives. This was not, however, just a reaction to contemporary pressures; they were also echoes of discussions central to the movement's origins, and they emanated from the ongoing strengths of the co-operative movement. While co-ops must constantly demonstrate their ability to meet business goals, they also function within specific contexts and historical traditions. They are steeped in the class, cultural, and ideological frameworks of their members and communities and they cannot escape them.

The Rochdale Pioneers, for example, envisioned creating colonies in the traditions of Robert Owen and his imitators; they were part of a working class culture and worldview that had been decades in formation. The consumer movements that emerged in their wake in many parts of the world, were not just concerned about purer and cheaper food, many within them were also "consumers against capitalism" (Furlough, Strikwerda, 1999). The worker co-ops that emerged in the nineteenth century, for example in France and Italy, were extensions of community activism based on co-operative, religious or political motivations. Many early financial co-ops emerged from community concerns and the dreams of individuals, like Friederich Raiffeisen, Leone Wollenborg, Alphonse Desjardins and Roy Bergengren, seeking to ameliorate them. It is a tradition still very much evident in credit union circles, for example, in support for Community Economic Development and in contributions to education and social programmes. The agricultural co-operatives that emerged in the nineteenth and early twentieth century in Europe, more recently in other parts of the world, reflected crises in rural life as market economics transformed the ways in which rural people live; they were concerned about women's and youth issues, rural education and rural culture.

The communitarian concerns of most co-operative endeavors in the North Atlantic world, so strong in the nineteenth and early twentieth century, tended to wither in the twentieth century for many reasons, in-cluding the complexity involved in meeting both economic and social purposes. The only managerial models readily available were drawn from the military, government and private business worlds. Within the co-op world, there were remarkable searches for alternative forms of management systems; for example, in some consumer wholesales, federated structures in the community banking movement, some agricultural organizations, the network systems of Northern Italy, worker-oriented movements as Mondragon, and the "co-op corporations" of Asia. Their distinctive ways, built out from co-operative thought and practice, how-ever, have never been fully studied or appreciated and they tended to lose their uniqueness as co-ops adapted to the market place. They tended to adopt "scissors and paste" management theory from other kinds of organisational behaviour rather than develop unique practices built out of co-operative values and principles.

The most serious challenge, in fact, came from the ascendancy of private enterprise models. A growing number of co-ops seemed content to follow the practices and conform to the values of their competitors, to be satisfied with being an "odd" variant of conventional business. Government officials, academics and business groups reinforced this trend, pro-claiming consciously and unconsciously the superiority of the investor driven firm and making it the yardstick by which co-ops would be measured.

At the same time, though, many governments did encourage new types of co-operative endeavour. For a few decades in the middle of the twentieth century, many governments were influenced by the prevailing economic orthodoxies provided by Keynesian economic theory and institutional economics. Keynesian models, for example, encouraged governments to support marketing and supply co-operatives and to use co-ops in building social safety nets. That kind of economic theory tended to lose out, however, in the seminar rooms of Economics Departments and in the halls of power within governments as the twentieth century ended. Indeed, to be taken seriously, co-ops had to stress their economic roles, pointing to their financial successes more than their social contributions in order to be respected by governments.

The communitarian perspective also lost out as co-ops curtailed their educational efforts. Many co-operative movements in the later nineteenth and early twentieth centuries possessed remarkable educational programmes, embracing a wide range of the media of the day and effectively building the movement. They used educational processes to en-courage diverse forms of co-operative enterprise, not just those in which they were directly engaged. As co-ops became pressed in their business activities and as their managements became increasingly "professional", however, they reduced their educational role, converting it to marketing and institutional promotion and lessening their community emphasis.

Finally, the co-operative "communitarian tradition" never achieved sufficient clarity and intellectual depth to be widely accepted, often collapsing into different kinds of socialist traditions, Marxist and Social Democrat, typically lumped together with them rather indiscriminately and unthinkingly. In a few places, it was even indistinguishable from anarchist collectivism.

Co-operative communitarianism is based on grassroots control and initiation and is committed to practicing reciprocity and mutuality. It exudes a kind of individualism that believes individual development is at least as dependent on group association as on individual initiative. Thought of institutionally, it sees enlightened individualism unfolding within a complex, often ambiguous set of relationships, including those associated with members, co-operative sectors, governments, and com-munities and reflected in daily management practice.

Thus, when the Manchester Congress addressed the social side of the international movement, it was resurrecting long held traditions of "community" but traditions that had faded in many established movements. It was also welcoming new co-operative forms through which people could control the social as well as the economic forces shaping their lives and their communal existence.

The Congress recaptured the social dimension of co-operatives in at least six ways: by inserting "cultural", "social needs" and "aspirations" in the definition it accepted (the first definition ever agreed to by the international movement); by including "social responsibility" and "caring for others" in the value statement; by concretely encouraging inclusive memberships approaches; by emphasizing member involvement and control, a characteristic that would naturally broaden co-op mandates; by emphasizing "common capital " rather than continuing the tendency to think of co-ops as mere agglomerations of members; and, of course, by specifying a commitment to "sustainable communities" in the seventh principle.

Since 1995 the international movement has continued to demonstrate a growing commitment to social goals. This has coincided with recent shifts in economic thought that recognize the importance of social capital and the value of such fields as Social and Environmental Economics. Moreover, as the role of the state has declined, new co-ops have emerged meeting social needs in health, elder care and care for people with disabilities. More generally, too, many co-ops have deepened their commitment to environmental protection, an acknowledgement of communal obligations. In almost every country, in fact, there are exciting new co-ops responding to social needs and opportunities derived from challenges facing communities.

There is, however, no simple road to enhanced social responsibility. Older, established co-operatives are significantly reflections of their traditions and are shaped by their memberships: they can expand possibilities incrementally, in a year-over-year fashion but they will not easily go through revolutionary reconstruction. The different kinds of established co-ops - consumer, farming, fishing, banking, worker and service - will identify possibilities in their own ways and according to the logic of their industries and their inheritance. New kinds of co-ops created in reaction to social possibilities will be more flexible, both in what they can do and in how they do it. There is a need to respect such diversity, not as easy as it might sound among co-operative people who can be quickly judge-mental and critical of those who do things differently.

There are also challenges about how to embed commitments, in both established and new co-operatives. The history of the international movement abounds with examples of discarded priorities and weakened resolution, particularly as co-ops "mature". Co-ops that started out with wide social visions have often become narrow in interests and limited in concerns.

Cooperatives in European Countries

Cooperative firms and social enterprises can, despite their differences, be interpreted in a unitary way as socially-oriented firms: they are entrepreneurial organizations that do not have as their main objective the maximization of private returns (net surpluses or profits) accruing to the investment of capital. Rather, cooperative firms are mutual benefit organizations that are usually controlled on an equal voting rights basis not by investors, but by different types of patrons (eg. producers, workers, consumers) or by a mix of them (multi-stakeholder cooperatives). They are created to protect first and foremost their members through the satisfaction of their needs, which can be private or social in nature. Social enterprises, as defined by the UK law on the Community Interest Company in 2005, and by the Italian law on the *Impresa Sociale* in 2006, are public-benefit organizations that pursue the satisfaction of social needs through the imposition of at least a partial non-profit constraint and by devoting the majority of their positive residuals and patrimony to socially-oriented activities. Their governance structure is similar to that of entrepreneurial non-profit organizations, as analyzed by the most specialized literature (Borzaga and Defourny, 2001).

Research concerning cooperatives and social enterprises is characterized by an increasingly evident contradiction between real phenomena, often confirmed by empirical research, and the contentions put forward, explicitly or otherwise, by the predominant theories. On the one hand, increasing evidence shows that such enterprises perform a significant and sometimes growing economic and social role in a variety of sectors and in many countries. As importantly, they often achieve economic and social outcomes that are better than those achieved by conventional enterprises and public institutions. The role played in the past twenty years by cooperatives and social enterprises in the production of innovative services of general interest, or the results achieved by credit cooperatives during the past ten years, and particularly during the recent financial crisis. On the other hand, the predominant theoretical approaches, primarily in economics, tend to underestimate these results and, consequently, the role and potential of this set of organizations (Ward, 1958; Furubotn and Pejovich, 1970; Hansmann, 1996). The positive role of cooperative and social enterprises is recognized only in limited cases—e.g., in Hansmann's (1996) work—and even when it is, the theory assigns these organizations a transitional role and relegates their relevance only to contexts characterized by severe market imperfections (such as lack of proper regulation and sufficient competition) and government failures (e.g. under-provision of public goods).

There are various reasons for this contradiction. First, many studies on cooperatives and social enterprises have been based on approaches that were too generic and ideological. For example, supporters of cooperatives and social enterprises have stressed solidarity, altruism and reciprocity as values informing the work of these organizations. These values are at the root of their democratic principles, and of the socialized nature of the added value they generate. However, values and ideology alone cannot explain the increasing economic and social role of cooperatives and social enterprises, or their efficiency and long-term sustainability. They also cannot be indistinguishably applied to all forms of cooperative and social enterprises (Borzaga and Tortia, 2010). Rather, a suitable interpretative framework is needed in order to properly evaluate their nature and their role in modern economic systems. The underestimation of the role of cooperative and social enterprises has also been reinforced by the difficulties in drawing general results from investigations and studies that frequently consider only specific sectors or geographical areas. The lack of shared objectives among researchers and specialized research institutions has hindered a coherent development of a doctrine and empirical research on these organizations. The predominant tendency has been to consider specific forms of cooperatives or social enterprises, often starting from highly specific research goals, with few attempts having been made to embed the analysis within broad and ambitious research designs. This has hampered the development of a general theory of these forms of enterprise that could stand comparison with the prevailing economic and social paradigms. Moreover, cooperatives and social enterprises are regulated by laws that differ greatly among countries, which makes any attempt to give them a sufficiently general interpretation (independent of national specificities) particularly complex.

However, the main reason for this undervaluation seems to be the difficulty of reconciling the features of these forms of enterprise with the hypotheses, if not the value judgments, underlying the dominant theories. In fact, the predominant economic, sociological and legal models developed during the 1900s (which underlie the institutions on which the modern economic and social systems are based) rely on a set of assumptions that include the prevalence of self-interested behaviour and the self-regulatory capacity of markets. These assumptions privilege institutional forms that are often incompatible with the ones that characterize cooperative and social enterprises. Not surprisingly, then, the dominant theories are unable to explain the emergence and evolution of these forms of enterprise and interpret their distinctive features.

Rural Credit Cooperatives in India

Rural Cooperative Banking and Credit Institutions play an important role in meeting the growing credit needs of rural India. The volume of credit flowing through these institutions has increased. The performance of these institutions, however (apparent in the share of total institutional credit and the indicators of their financial health), has been less than satisfactory and is deteriorating rapidly. Of late, a number of Committees have gone into the reasons for this situation and suggested remedial measures, but there has been little progress in implementing their recommendations.

Apart from relying on the findings of the earlier committees, the Task Force also collected substantial statistical data on the coverage and financial aspects of cooperative credit institutions from published and readily available sources. It also analyzed these data to highlight differences across and within States in performance indicators and trends therein. The Task Force also sought to collect information on selected aspects of their governance, through the regional and district offices of the National Bank for Agriculture and Rural Development (NABARD).

The Task Force also had extensive discussions with senior officials of State Cooperation Departments, managers and chief executives of cooperative credit societies, leading cooperators with deep involvement and experience in the cooperative movement, representatives of trade unions of employees of cooperatives, apart from academics and non government organizations (NGOs) well versed on cooperative credit.

These consultations were held to ascertain their perceptions and views on the current status of cooperatives, including issues relating to governance and management, the role of the State Governments and the extent of their intrusion or otherwise, into the affairs of the cooperatives. The Task Force invited their views on factors that have impeded cooperatives from becoming autonomous and member driven institutions, and the strategy for their revival and revitalization. During the eight meetings held in different parts of the country, the Task Force was able to exchange views with about 150 cooperators, academics officials etc., from as many as 23 States. A number of organizations also sent in written memoranda.

The inputs from this sub group and a special consultation with officials and non-officials with firsthand knowledge of cooperative law, its administration and problems in changing the law, have been invaluable to the Task Force in clarifying its understanding of the issues involved, and in helping to formulate its recommendations.

Evolution of Cooperative Finance

The First Phase: 1900-1930

By the beginning of the 20th Century, officials of the colonial government perceived the Indian farmers' dependence on usurious moneylenders to be a major cause of their indebtedness and poverty. At that time the cooperative movement had become well established in Europe and achieved remarkable success there. Convinced that the cooperative movement offered the best means of liberating Indian farmers from the crushing burden of debt and the tyranny of moneylenders, Indian officials began to take active interest in promoting credit cooperatives in the country. Societies were organized for the first time in the closing years of the 19th Century.

The passage of the Cooperative Credit Societies Act in 1904, and the enactment of a more comprehensive Cooperative Societies Act in 1912 marked the beginning of a government policy of active encouragement and promotion of cooperatives. This thinking gained wide acceptance and was adopted as a policy by provincial governments and thereafter, "cooperation" became a provincial subject in 1919. The persistence of government interest in cooperatives and the importance attached to them was reflected in the appointment of three different Committees to review their growth and functioning.

The classic study by Frederic Nicholson, followed by the Edward Law Committee on Cooperative Legislation, confirmed and reiterated the need for the State to actively promote cooperatives. A decade later, the Maclagan Committee (1915) advocated that "there should be one cooperative for every village and every village should be covered by a cooperative". The Royal Commission on Agriculture in India, which submitted its report in 1928, suggested among other things, that the cooperative movement should continue to focus on expanding rural credit and that the State should patronize cooperatives and protect the sector.

It was the Royal Commission which made the observation "if cooperation fails, there will fail the best hope of rural India". By this time, the State was already deeply involved in promoting agricultural credit cooperatives. The number of societies reached impressive proportions and diversified their activities well beyond agricultural credit. Debates centered on whether or not each village should have a cooperative and whether there should be a single purpose or a multi-purpose cooperative at the village level.

The Second Phase: 1930-1950

The major development during this phase was the role played by the Reserve Bank of India (RBI). The Reserve Bank's concern and involvement in the sphere of rural credit stemmed from its very statute of incorporation. Specific provisions were made in the Reserve Bank of India Act, 1934 both for the establishment of an Agricultural Credit Department (ACD) in the bank and for extending refinance facilities to the cooperative credit system. Emphasis was laid on setting up, strengthening and promoting financially viable provincial cooperative banks, central cooperative banks, marketing societies and primary agricultural credit societies in each province. The RBI, since 1942, also started extending credit facilities to provincial cooperative banks for seasonal agricultural operations and marketing of crops.

The Government policy during this phase was not as pro-active on promoting cooperatives as before. There seemed to be a policy lull until 1945, when the Agricultural Finance Sub-committee and the Cooperative Planning Committee were set up by the Government of India (GoI). By then, there already were signs of sickness in the Indian rural cooperative movement. A large number of cooperatives were found to be saddled with the problem of frozen assets, because of heavy overdues in repayment. The Sub-committee's recommendation that the frozen assets of the members of such cooperatives be liquidated, by adjusting the claims of the society to the repaying capacity of the members, marked the beginning of State interference in the management of cooperatives and the consequent erosion in the credit discipline of the members. The Cooperative Planning Committee identified the small size of the primary cooperative as the principal cause of failure. It also advocated State protection to the cooperative sector from competition.

The Third Phase: 1950–1990

After Independence, rapid and equitable economic development became the central focus of State policy. Cooperatives in general, and rural financial cooperatives in particular, were once again on centre stage. Taking cognizance of the weakness of the cooperative system, the All India Rural Credit Survey (AIRCS) not only recommended State partnership in terms of equity, but also partnership in terms of governance and management. Other recommendations included linking credit and marketing cooperatives and enlarging their area of operation. The recommendations of the AIRCS stopped just short of the Government running the cooperatives, and paved the way for its direct intrusion in the governance and management of cooperatives. State policy came to be premised on the view that the government should ensure adequate supply of cheap institutional credit to rural areas through cooperatives. The thinking then was that if the institutions that were meant to deliver such cheap institutional credit failed, there either had to be reorganization of existing institutions, or creation of new types of institutions. The Hazari Committee recommended integration of short term and long term structures. The Bawa Committee (1971) recommended setting up Large Multi-purpose Cooperatives in tribal areas. The National Commission on Agriculture (1976) recommended setting up Farmers Service Cooperative Societies with the active collaboration of the nationalized banks.

NABARD was created on the recommendation of the CRAFICARD (Silverman Committee 1981). The State's heightened interest in and concern for the performance of cooperatives in the country was obvious. The focus, however, was on expanding and reorganizing the State supported structures, without addressing the tasks of restoring and strengthening autonomy, mutual help and self-governance that are the cornerstones of genuine cooperatives.

The State gave primacy to cooperatives as the sole means of delivering institutional credit to rural areas and injected large and increasing amounts of funds directly. Upper tier cooperative banks were encouraged to accept public deposits and borrow from other financial institutions. However, the system was soon found to be burdened by growing overdues. In keeping with the national priority of financing the rural sector adequately, the involvement of commercial banks was first suggested as a social control measure. The involvement of commercial banks was thereafter institutionalized through the nationalization of major commercial banks in 1969. During the post-nationalization period, there was an unprecedented penetration of commercial banks in the rural sector. This trend, however, was accompanied by rigid policy directives right down to the micro level on cost of credit, purposes, categories of borrowers, geographical areas, etc.

As the financial involvement of the government in cooperatives increased, its interference in all aspects of the functioning of cooperatives also increased. The consequent interference with the functioning of the co-operative institutions, often compelling them to compromise on the usual norms for credit worthiness, ultimately began to affect the quality of the portfolio of the cooperatives.

Instead of tackling the root cause of their weaknesses, the State took responsibility for strengthening the institutions, by infusing additional capital and "professional" workforce. Both the State and the workforce then began to behave like "patrons", rather than as providers of financial services. Whenever any professional organization is in trouble, it usually finds its own solution by re-negotiating the terms with its financiers and re-visiting its operating strategies. However, in the case of the rural financial institutions, the State has always provided a "solution", irrespective of the need of the recipient organization, thereby donning the role of a "patron".

In due course, political expediency also led to laxity in ensuring quality of credit and its repayment. The Government of India's 1989 scheme for writing off loans of farmers, greatly aggravated the already weak credit discipline in the cooperative system and led to the erosion of its financial health. It also set up an unhealthy precedent and spawned a series of schemes by the State Governments, announcing waivers of various magnitudes, ranging from interest write off to partial loan write-offs. The competitive populism adopted by the political class has severely impaired the credibility and health of the cooperative credit structure.

The State has used co-operatives to channel its development schemes, particularly subsidy-based programmers for the poor. As these institutions have a wide reach in the rural areas and also deal with finances, the choice was natural. The trend, however, also made cooperatives a conduit for distributing political patronage. This and the sheer magnitude of resources and benefits channeled through the societies, makes control of decision-making and management attractive to parties in power, for accommodating their members, to influence decisions through directives, and for individual politicians to be on the management boards of the cooperatives.

Concerns about these trends and the need to overcome them began to be voiced around this time. The Agriculture Credit Review Committee (Khusro Committee, 1989) for the first time, talked of the importance of encouraging members' thrift and savings for the cooperatives. It also emphasised the need for better business planning at the local level and for strategies to enable cooperatives to be self-sustaining. To this end, the Committee was also in favour of serving non-members, if it made business sense. In a sense, there were larger macro-economic changes on the anvil in the economy. The 1990s witnessed more concerted attempts both by the government and by non-official organizations and cooperators, to explore ways to revitalise the cooperatives.

The Fourth Phase: 1990s and Onwards

During the last fifteen years, there has been an increasing realization of the destructive effects of intrusive State patronage, politicization, and the consequent impairment of the role of cooperatives in general, and of credit cooperatives in particular, leading to a quest for reviving and revitalizing the cooperative movement.

Several Committees (notably those headed by Chaudhry Brahm Perkash, Jagdish Capoor, Vikhe Patil and V S Vyas) were set up to suggest cooperative sector reforms during this period. The Brahm Perkash Committee emphasized the need to make cooperatives self-reliant, autonomous and fully democratic institutions and proposed a Model Law. Subsequent Committees have all endorsed this recommendation and strongly supported replacing existing laws with the proposed Model Law. They have also recommended revamping and streamlining the regulation and supervision mechanism, introducing prudential norms and bringing cooperative banks fully under the ambit of the Banking Regulation Act, 1949. To facilitate the implementation of these reforms, they proposed that governments provide viable cooperative credit institutions with financial assistance for recapitalization.

Progress in implementing these suggestions has been very tardy because of the States' unwillingness to share in costs and their reluctance to dilute their powers and to cede regulatory powers to the Reserve Bank of India (RBI). The passage of the Mutually Aided Cooperative Societies Act by the Andhra Pradesh government in 1995, however, marked a significant step towards reform. Following the example of Andhra Pradesh, eight other States (viz., Bihar, Chhattisgarh, Jammu and Kashmir, Jharkhand, Karnataka, Madhya Pradesh, Orissa and Uttaranchal) have passed similar legislation to govern and regulate mutually aided cooperatives.

In all cases these new laws provide for cooperatives to be democratic, self-reliant and member-centric, without any State involvement or financial support. They provide for cooperatives registered under the old law to migrate to the new Act. The old Acts were not repealed, nor was there any serious effort to encourage and facilitate the conversion of old cooperatives to come within the purview of the new Act. Most existing cooperatives, therefore, continued to adhere to the old law.

The new law, however, did lead to the emergence of a "new generation autonomous financial cooperatives", albeit slowly and unevenly across the country. While the number of cooperatives registered under the new liberal Act is slowly picking up, the conversion from the old law to the new Act has largely been in the arena of commodity cooperatives. The reason for the slow pace at which both credit cooperatives and the primary agricultural credit societies (PACS) are adopting the new law is largely because they are not eligible for refinance under the existing legal and structural arrangements.

As will be evident from the next chapter, these developments have not made much of an impact on the way cooperatives function. The movement has continued to deteriorate and reached the point that necessitated the appointment of the present Task Force, which has been entrusted with the task of coming up with an implementable action plan for carrying the reforms forward.

Implementation Mechanism

The NABARD will guide the field level implementation teams in approving bank specific restructuring programmes, enter into agreements with individual banks covering the terms and conditions of the programmes, and follow up its progress with the bank and other concerned agencies. Among other things, it will also have the authority to operate the Funds earmarked by the GoI and ensure its proper use. To provide overall guidance and to monitor the progress of the process at the national and State levels, however, it is necessary to have independent committees of stakeholders with defined responsibilities.

At the national level, there would be a National Guidance and Monitoring Committee. This committee will be chaired by Secretary (FS), GoI, and will include as its members Additional Secretary, Ministry of Agriculture, GoI, Chairman, NABARD, two eminent cooperators, one representative from the Reserve Bank of India (RBI) and one representative from the State under review. This Committee will act as the clearing house for policy references and monitor the implementation of the Scheme, on an All India basis.

The National Committee will report to the Finance Minister on a quarterly basis. A dedicated team in NABARD's headquarters (HQs) will support this committee. The secretariat to the committee will also be provided by NABARD.

At the field level, i.e., at the level of the PACS, DCCBs and SCBs, the programme will be implemented by a two tier structure, one at the State level and the second at the district level.

State Level

A State level Implementation and Monitoring Committee will be put in position with Secretary, Finance (State Government), as Chairman and Secretary, Cooperation (State Government), Executive Director, NABARD, State RCS, MD, SCB and a chartered accountant as members. The task to be attended by this Committee will include, signing an MOU between the State Government, SCB, DCCBs and the RBI, ensuring drawing up of balance sheet and its vetting, assessment of financial assistance required at SCB level, recommending release of assistance on fulfillment of the prescribed conditionalities, and overall supervision and control of the implementation of the scheme in the State. A dedicated team in the NABARD regional office will assist this Committee.

District Level

A district level Planning and Implementation Committee, working under the overall guidance and supervision of the State Level Committee, would be set up in each district. Each district committee would be chaired by NABARD and comprise representatives of the State Government, the concerned DCCB, and a Chartered Accountant. Their work will relate to ensuring conduct of special audit as on March 2004 for all PACS and the DCCB, drawing up and vetting of balance sheets of these PACS and DCCB, getting MOUs signed, institution-wise assessment of financial assistance required, recommending release of such assistance on fulfillment of the prescribed conditionalities and overseeing implementation.

The committee will also ensure establishing and stabilizing of accounting systems, MIS, and computerization, and required HRD over a period of two years. A two or three member team of dedicated officers, drawn from NABARD or contracted especially for the purpose, and working full time on implementation of the Revival Package (RP) will support the Committee.

Role of NABARD

The NABARD will prepare model MOUs, model balance sheet preformed for PACS and DCCBs, get accounting systems designed, get common software and hardware plan prepared, and design training modules and manuals. All implementation costs, including costs of dedicated teams at the district, State and national levels, will be fully met through GoI grant support.

Implementation Time frame

Once the GoI announces the scheme, it is expected that some States may agree to participate immediately, while some others may do so later. Similarly, CCS units may also take some time to true their balance sheets as on March 2004. The implementation of the scheme is, therefore, likely to be staggered in different States. It is expected that the process, once started in any State, will take between two to three years to complete all the stages of legal and institutional reforms, capitalization, and institutional ,human resources capacity building.

There is increasing recognition within India's central and state governments about the usefulness of engaging or facilitating the private sector to address some of the country's pressing developmental needs, although the specific nomenclature of "social enterprises" is not often used. The Government has been involved in three main categories: Micro, Small, and Medium Enterprises (MSMEs) engagement, government-backed venture capital funds, and policy formulation.

First, the government has initiated various public–private partnerships in key development sectors, such as health. For example, many state governments have invited private sector players to provide emergency health care services in urban areas. MSMEs have been identified as a priority lending sector. This increases the availability of capital through government provisioning of grants, equity, and subsidized loans for companies in this category. This clustering includes all enterprises with an initial outlay below $2 million. Since almost all for-profit SEs fall into this category, they will benefit from this policy. Recently, the Prime Minister of India also commissioned a special task force to provide a set of recommendations on further developing India's MSMEs. The task force recommended that the government should spend around $1.1 billion over the next 3 to 5 years on augmenting infrastructure and technological support for MSMEs; of these funds, around 20% should be earmarked for incubation centers within reputable educational institutions. Secondly, the National Innovation Council, set up by the Prime Minister in 2010 to catalyze innovation in India, is considering establishment of a government-backed venture capital fund. The size of this fund will be in the ballpark of $200 million.

The primary focus of this fund would be to address developmental needs in education, health, infrastructure, and sanitation. Thirdly, the government is involved in formulating and changing policies and regulations that can affect the SE space. Most recently, the Securities and Exchange Board of India (SEBI), the country's financial market regulator, floated a policy paper suggesting the need to separately recognize and regulate "Social Venture Funds". It outlined that these funds are for investors seeking "muted" returns in their investments in return for social gains. SEBI sought public comments on its note and the final recommendations are yet to be finalized.

Need for Cooperative Entrepreneurship Development System in Current Scenario

Effects of Economic Liberalization

We have seen landmark shift in Indian Economy since the adoption of new economic policy in 1991. This had far reaching impacts on all spheres of life in India. There can be no concrete conclusions about their impact on Indian people. This turns out to be more of an ideological debate like capitalism vs Socialism. But there is no doubt in the fact that those reforms were unavoidable and very compelling. There was in fact, similar wave all across the globe after disintegration of USSR and end of the Cold War. Many Post-colonial democratic regimes, which were earlier sheltered by USSR, lost their umbrella. They had no option, but to fall in line to new unipolar world order dictated by USA. Even China in late 1980's adopted 'Open Door Policy' through which it liberalized its economy by shedding communist mentality completely. South East Asian economies also reformed their economy and started engaging more with global economy. These along with China, pursued export led growth whereas Indian economy still relies almost wholly on domestic consumption.

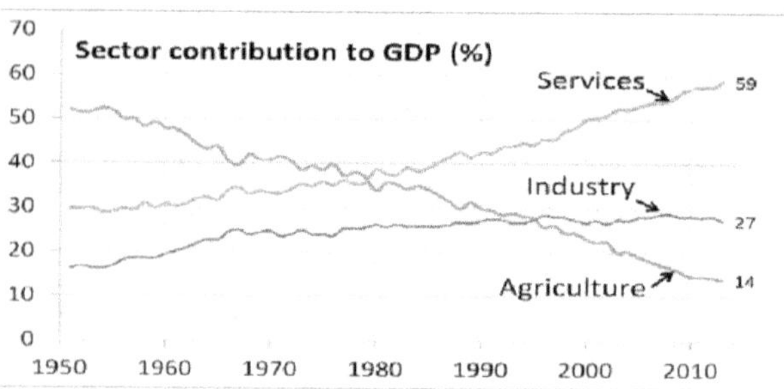

Patterns in the above graph explain inequity of Indian growth story. As per principle of economics, when a particular sector performs disproportionately higher than average growth rate, economic wealth starts concentrating into that sector. In this case that sector is Service sector. Within this sector, highest growth is marked by sectors such as financial services, Real estate services etc. , which are least employment elastic. Consequently, Growth of past decade was limited to upscale areas of the countries as almost whole service industry, operates from these areas. Majority of India got spillover or trickle down growth from here. This accelerated migration to urban areas. This in turned created array of social problems associated with urbanization. It fundamentally changed pattern of Indian Society.

Now we have ultra-modern and ultra-primitive society coexisting and conflicting with each other. On one side Social institutions like Personal Law boards, Khaps & kangaroo courts etc. tries to uphold their control over their respective community members, on other hand there is western wave pulling out these very members.

Undoubtedly strongest revolution of new century has been one of Information Technology, which started in last years of past century. This revolution was different because it made globalization even more obvious and stark. It made possible transfer of real time human labor across nations, without transfer humans themselves. Further, it erased all boundaries which hinder free flow of information. This has benefited sharing, nurturing and development of knowledge in societies which earlier had access only to substandard or non-updated information. As always package is coupled with some grim realities too.

Governments all across the world has lost their capacity to regulate and ward of against malicious, false, sensitive information and content. Rise of Islamic State demonstrates that, IT revolution has helped development of global Terrorist links more than anything. Moreover, explicit content is freely available on web, to which unmatured children have unrestricted access

GDP growth rate: India's annual average growth rate from 1990 – 2010 has been 6.6 % which is almost double than pre reforms era. GDP growth rate surpassed 5% mark in early 1980's. This made impact of 1990's reforms on growth unclear. Some believe that 1980's reforms were precursor to LPG reforms. Other things apart, it is clear that 1980 reforms led to crash of economy in 1991, which was remedied by LPG reforms which were quite more comprehensive. It was IMF loan which gave government to adjust its economy. It was largest ever loan given by IMF. Initially there were global doubts on India's credibility for loan, but India has been so far a disciplined borrower.

Industrial Growth Rate: Barring few years industrial growth rate has been not much impressive. Share of Industry still remains stagnantly low at 25%. Worst is that India has transitioned to be a service led economy, directly from an agrarian one. One expiation of this is end of policy of imports substitution which derived industrial growth upto 1990. Foreign companies got free access to Indian markets and made domestic products uncompetitive. They obviously had better access to technology and larger economies of scale.

India's position also lagged on account of Research and innovation. Import substitution required certain degree of investment and efforts in domestic production. It was carried out even when imports were cheaper. This resulted in good and better capacity building upto that time. This was coupled with constant technology denial by west, which further pushed government to spend on R&D. Technology Denial ended with liberalization and globalization. Till that time Indian Industry was better and modern than that of China. But in two decades China has surpassed India by huge margin in case of both Industry and innovation.

Impact on Small Scale in India

This impact shall be studied right from the beginning of colonization in 18th century. Colonization can be considered as 1st wave of globalization. In pre colonization era, India's textiles and handicraft was renowned worldwide and was backbone of Indian economy. With coming of industrial revolution along with foreign rule in India, Indian economy suffered a major setback and much of its indigenous small scale cottage Industry was destroyed.

After independence, government attempted to revive small scale sector by reserving items exclusively for it to manufacture. With liberalization list of reserved items was substantially curtailed and many new sectors were thrown open to big players.

Small scale industry however exists and still remains backbone of Indian Economy. It contributes to major portion of exports and private sector employment. Results are mixed, many erstwhile Small scale industries got bigger and better. But overall value addition, product innovation and technology adoption remains dismal and they exist only on back of government support. Their products are contested by cheaper imports from China. Policies of government toward SSI were covered in previous article access here and here

Impact on Agriculture

As already said, share of agriculture in domestic economy has declined to about 15%. However, people dependent upon agriculture are still around 55%. Cropping patterns has undergone a huge change, but impact of liberalization can't be properly assessed.

We saw under series relating to agriculture that there are still all pervasive government controls and interventions starting from production to distribution (here SPS and here – WTO).

Global agricultural economy is highly distorted. This is mainly because imbalance in economic and political power in hands of farmers of developed and developing countries. In developed countries, commercial and capitalistic agriculture is in place which is owned by influential Agri corporations. They easily influence policies of WTO and extract a better deal for themselves at cost of farmers of developing world.

Farming in developing world is subsistence and supports large number of poor people. With globalization there has been high fluctuation in commodity prices which put them in massive risk. This is particularly true for cash crops like Cotton and Sugarcane. Recent crises in both crops indicate towards this conclusively.

Also there is global Food vs. Fuel confusion going on. Sugar and corn are used to manufacture ethanol which is used as fuel. In USA Corn is produced mainly for this purpose, as sugar cane is in Brazil. Now there are apprehensions that what if converting food into fuel is more remunerative for producers? More than 1 billion people still live in hunger, much more are just hand to mouth.

It is futile to expect that free market will take care of these people, who don't have any purchasing power. Clearly, Agriculture is biggest market failure, but is rarely discussed for being so in WTO.

Another global debate born out of globalization is one of GM crops. Here too powerful MNCs like Monsanto hold the key. USA allows unhindered use of GM crops, but EU bans it. In India field trails are going on. (It was discusses here)

On the positive note, India's largely self-sufficient and high value distinguished products like Basmati Rice are in high demand all over. Generally speaking, India is better placed to take up challenge of globalization in this case. If done in sustainable and inclusive manner, it will have a huge multiplier impact on whole economy. Worldwide implicit compulsion to develop Food processing Industry is another landmark effect of globalization.

Apart from these, Farm Mechanization i.e. use of electronic/solar pumps, Tractors, combines etc. all are fruits of globalization. Now moving a step further, Information technology is being incorporated into agriculture to facilitate farming.

Impact on Services Sector

In this case globalization has been boon for developing countries and bane for developed ones. Due to historic economic disparity between two groups, human resources have been much cheaper in developing economies. This was further facilitated by IT revolution and this all culminated in exodus of numerous jobs from developed countries to developing countries. Here US have to jealously guard its jobs as we guard our agriculture.

IT Industry

Software, BPO, KPO, LPO industry boom in India has helped India to absorb a big chunk of demographic dividend, which otherwise could have wasted. Best part is that export of services result in export of high value. There is almost no material exported which consume some natural resource. Only thing exported is labor of Professionals, which doesn't deplete, instead grows with time. Now India is better placed to become a truly Knowledge Economy.

Exports of these services constitute big part of India's foreign Exchange earnings. In fact, the only three years India had Current Account surplus, I.e. 2000-2002, was on back of this export only.

Banking

Further, in banking too India has been a gainer. Since reforms, there have been three rounds of License Grants for private banks. Private Banks such as ICICI, HDFC, Yes Bank and also foreign banks, raised standards of Indian Banking Industry. Now there is cut through competition in the banking industry, and public sector banks are more responsive to customers.

Here too IT is on path of bringing banking revolution. New government schemes like Pradhan Mantri Jan dhan Yojana aims to achieve their targets by using Adhaar Card. Having said this, Public Sector Banks still remain major lender in the country.

Similarly Insurance Industry now offers variety of products such as Unit Linked Insurance plans, Travel Insurance etc. But, in India life Insurance business is still decisively in hands of Life Insurance Corporation of India.

Stock Markets

Another major development is one of Stock Markets. Stock Markets are platforms on which Corporate Securities can be traded real time. It provides mechanisms for constant price discovery, options for investors to exit from or enter into investment any time.

These are back bone of free markets these days and there is robust trade going all over the world on stock exchanges. Their Importance can be estimated from the fact that, behavior of stock markets of a country is strongest indicator of health and future prospects of an economy.

These markets has thrown open wide array of associated services such as Investment Banking, Asset Management, Underwriting services, Hedging advice etc. These collectively employ lakhs of people all over India.

Similarly there are commodities market which provides avenues for investment and sale of various eligible commodities.

Telecom Sector

Conventionally, Telecom sector was a government owned monopoly and consequently service was quite substandard. After reforms, private telecom sector reached pinnacle of success. And Indian telecom companies went global. However, corruption and rent seeking marred growth and outlook of this sector.

Entry of modern **Direct to Home** services saw improvements in quality of Television services on one hand and loss of livelihood for numerous local cable operators.

Education and Health Sector

It should be noted that food (Agriculture), Health and education (and to lesser extent banking) are among basic necessities, which every human being deserves and can't do without. Unfortunately, in developing countries there is market failure in all these sectors and majority of people can't afford beyond a certain limit (or can't afford at all). Concept of free markets, globalization, liberalization etc. fails here miserably. Free markets provide goods and services to people who can afford paying for them, not to those who deserve and need these.

Now if we consider these sectors from angle of our inclination towards free markets, certainly there has been lot of progress. There has been world class education available in India and Deregulation has resulted in Mushrooming of private engineering and Medical Colleges. But in reality, this had far reaching devastating effect on society.

These new colleges accommodate only a miniscule proportion of aspirants at very high costs. Recently, an Independent organization 'Transparency International' came out with report claiming that India's medical system is most corrupt in the world. This was no surprise, we all know from where it starts. High fees of education forces many aspirants to take educational loans from banks. After qualifying job market is unable to absorb majority of them. Practice turns out to be option of last resort. Now to make a decent living and to pay back the loans person is lured by corruption. Consequently, when many similar cases are put together, we get a corrupt system, economy and society.

Reality is that after deregulation and liberalization, government along with other sectors, pulled its hand from social sectors too. Now there is Mediocre to high quality options are available in private sector which can be availed as per one's budget. In public Sector Less than Mediocre to Mediocre options are available. This leaves huge proportion of aspiring students and expecting patients.

On Social front India's performance is deplored all over the world and it is probably behind all important developing economies. This lacuna has been recognized and government has taken the charge. In case of education almost universal enrollments has been achieved upto primary level and now impetus should be on improving quality, so that student of public schools comes at par with at least average private ones.

CHAPTER-II

INDIA'S ECONOMIC REFORMS

Reforms in Industrial Policy

Industrial policy was restructured to a great extent and most of the central government industrial controls were dismantled. Massive deregulation of the industrial sector was done in order to bring in the element of competition and increase efficiency. Industrial licensing by the central government was almost abolished except for a few hazardous and environmentally sensitive industries. The list of industries reserved solely for the public sector-which used to cover 18 industries, including iron and steel, heavy plant and machinery, telecommunications and telecom equipment, minerals, oil, mining, air transport services and electricity generation and distribution was drastically reduced to three: defense aircrafts and warships, atomic energy generation, and railway transport. Further, restrictions that existed on the import of foreign technology were withdrawn.

Reforms in Trade Policy

It was realized that the import substituting inward looking development policy was no longer suitable in the modern globalizing world.

Before the reforms, trade policy was characterized by high tariffs and pervasive import restrictions. Imports of manufactured consumer goods were completely banned. For capital goods, raw materials and intermediates, certain lists of goods were freely importable, but for most items where domestic substitutes were being produced, imports were only possible with import licenses.

The criteria for issue of licenses were non-transparent, delays were endemic and corruption unavoidable. The economic reforms sought to phase out import licensing and also to reduce import duties.

Import licensing was abolished relatively early for capital goods and intermediates which became freely importable in 1993, simultaneously with the switch to a flexible exchange rate regime. Quantitative restrictions on imports of manufactured consumer goods and agricultural products were finally removed on April 1, 2001, almost exactly ten years after the reforms began, and that in part because of a ruling by a World Trade Organization dispute panel on a complaint brought by the United States.

Financial Sector Reforms

Financial sector reforms have long been regarded as an integral part of the overall policy reforms in India. India has recognized that these reforms are imperative for increasing the efficiency of resource mobilization and allocation in the real economy and for the overall macroeconomic stability. The reforms have been driven by a thrust towards liberalization and several initiatives such as liberalization in the interest rate and reserve requirements have been taken on this front. At the same time, the government has emphasized on stronger regulation aimed at strengthening prudential norms, transparency and supervision to mitigate the prospects of systemic risks. Today the Indian financial structure is inherently strong, functionally diverse, efficient and globally competitive. During the last fifteen years, the Indian financial system has been incrementally deregulated and exposed to international financial markets along with the introduction of new instruments and products.

Agriculture Issue by Economic Reforms

Agriculture in India was assigned to one of the lower castes in the Hindu hierarchy. The villages had poor infrastructure; farmers used age-old traditional technology within the limits of local inputs and found customers for the surplus produce within the village and in the nearby markets. Vagaries of monsoons, tyranny of the kings and the brutalities of the invaders made investment in Agriculture highly hazardous.

The farmers as a community remained impoverished, indebted and bound by the very strict edicts of their community and by traditions. The British Rule brought Law and Order but worsened the immiseration. It also brought the first dawn of liberalization from ignorance and traditions.

Second Liberation

The early farmers movements were aimed against the tyranny of the landlords and the money-lenders. The peasants' revolts erupted as and when provocation arose and calmed down pretty soon. After independence, the system of landlords was abolished and the money-lenders were replaced by co-operative banks. The peasantry experienced a second liberation – this time from the local tyranny.

Anti-farmer Price Policies

The agriculture continued to be a non-paying proposition due to the anti-farmer price policies of the government restricting movement, transport, storage and marketing of agricultural produce. The poverty and the indebtedness continued.

Most of the farm organizations demanded help and subsidies. A major stream, however, demanded a free agricultural economy in a free national economic system.

Agriculture Untouched by Economic Reforms

In 1991, when the nehruvian socialistic pattern collapsed, Indian industry was the most subsidized in the world, while the Agriculture in India was the most taxed. The Economic Reforms of the 1991 vintage should have addressed themselves to the problem of this duality and to providing Indian farmers' freedom of access to markets and technology. In fact, they barely touched agriculture. The Economic Reforms remained, largely, confined to the non-agricultural sector. Despite the fact that India continues to be principally primary producer country, globalization is considered to be relevant only in the non-farm sector. The application of policies to liberalize as also to globalize Indian agriculture calls for a detailed study.

Liberalization in Indian Agriculture

That the Economic reforms in India have largely bypassed agriculture is largely conceded. There is, however, little realization that agriculture never was on the agenda of the Economic Reforms (ER). For its architects, ER consist essentially of creating an economic environment combining the discipline of competitive markets with efficient public services. Sustained and broad based agricultural development was, in the eyes of its authors, necessary for ER but only in order to alleviate rural poverty, assure food security, generate a buoyant market and contribute to export effort.

The agricultural base for ER was to be developed through, not competitive market environment as in the non-agrarian sector, but through the old familiar public investments, upkeep of infrastructure, maintenance of remunerative prices, reinforcement of land and tenure reforms, promotion of agro-processing, improvement of rural credit and R&D etc. The only innovations were to be scaling down of preferential protection to industries, de-restriction of domestic trade, relaxation of export controls and curtailment of the regime of so called `farm subsidies'.

Reverse Order

That the draft National Agricultural Policy Resolution (1995) should be totally untouched by the winds of ER, the leaders of Indian ER consider Agriculture to be out of its bounds. Countries like China ushered in reforms first in agriculture and then carried it through industry and trade. That India is following opposite strategy is not an oversight or omission but a deliberate act of commission.

Indian Dualism

ER came in most third world countries to correct the excesses of command economies with planning, priority for public sector and industrialization and protectionism. In India, the old system had yet another feature – dualism. Indian industry had the world's highest level of protection while the agricultural sector suffered under the most insufferable burden of negative subsidies.

The ER in India should have aimed at correcting both the statism and the dualism of the post-independence epoch. In fact, ER should have been ushered in agriculture with over-riding priority, given that the farm sector was in a far better position to take advantage of both, liberalization and globalization.

Following upon the devaluation of the Rupee (1992), the agricultural sector demonstrated its potential for entering export market. The ER continue, nevertheless, to circumvent the agricultural sector.

Convertibility

The progressive convertibility on the current account has left the agriculture unaffected because of the highly restrictive export-import regime.

The only noticeable investment in Indian agriculture from outside has been in the field of agro-processing and to a lesser extent, in the area of soft technology. Fertilizers, pesticides, plant and machinery have attracted little attention from the investors abroad on account of the restrictive licensing regime.

Delicensing

The delicensing so much talked about has barely touched agriculture or its backward and forward linkages. Fertilizers, sugar, alcohol, milk-processing, molasses, cotton-ginning, rice-milling — all continue under licensing systems.

Paddy is subject to compulsory levy all over the country and to monopoly state procurement in the tribal areas; cotton is under monopoly state control in Maharashtra; 40% of sugar produced is taken by the State at low prices; edible oil is subject to market intervention operation. The draconian Essential Commodities Act still rules. The monopoly powers of the Agricultural Produce Marketing Committees have remained intact despite ER.

The omnibus and amorphous Public Distribution System, despite its demonstrated inefficiency, wastefulness and corruption, continues in clear breach of the regulations of the World Trade Organisation (WTO).

Exim Restrictions

Most agricultural commodities continue to be under severe export bans, controls and quotas, which are operated in a manner that would effectively destroy any chance of building up a sustained international market, e.g. cotton, onions, sugar.

There are any number of instances of wilful dumping by the Central Government through non-commercial imports causing serious uncertainty. This has been particularly so in sugar, edible oil and wheat.

Subsidies

The authors of ER share the leftist misunderstanding that the farm sector has been benefiting from massive subsidies, particularly as regards subsidies on food, fertilizers, electricity, and water. They were, therefore, led to a self-contradictory argument that slashing of these subsidies and utilization of the funds thus saved for investment in agriculture is the best way of capitalization in agriculture. The fact has been that the real beneficiaries of these subsidies have been communities other than farmers and that the farmers all along have suffered from heavy negative subsidies. For quite some time the prospects of an impending income tax on agriculture are being suggested.

Negative Subsidy

The Ministry of Commerce has revealed in connection with the WTO Agreement that the farm sector had a hefty product-specific negative subsidy of over Rs. 1,13000 crores in respect of just 17 commodities amounting to 87% of the total value of production. As against this the non-product-specific subsidies on account of electricity, water, fertilizers etc. benefiting agriculture does not exceed Rs. 12,000 crores per year. Thus, even the knowledgeable people talk of the need to slash the farm subsidies and to impose agricultural income tax in the name of equity as if they knew not that the farm sector has a turnover tax of over 87%.

Property Rights

In the Economic Survey 1992-93, the need to promote consolidation of fragmented land holding with a view to meet the challenge of export market was underlined. There has been no follow-up.

The fragmentation has resulted from a plethora of Zamindari, Tenancy, Ceiling and Acquisition Acts adopted under the then popular notion that land reform is the first step to development.

These unconstitutional legislations were supported by successive amendments to the Constitution culminating in abolition of the fundamental right to property and in the birth of the atrocious Ninth Schedule putting hundreds of legislations beyond the purview of judicial review. Abolition of the peremptory acquisition powers and restoration of the fundamental right to property should have been high on the priority list of ER. In fact, no steps have been taken, howsoever.

Further, all measures taken for redistribution of agricultural land without any counterpart action in the urban non-agricultural sector need to be reviewed. The distinction between agricultural and non-agricultural lands as revenue categories needs to be removed.

Co-operatives

Since 1951, the Co-operatives as a form of business organization has been exploited for political purposes with the result that bureaucratic controls, corruption and inefficiency has made most co-operatives uneconomic organizations that can not withstand competition. The hefty subsidies they receive represent a serious handicap to emerging genuine non-political entrepreneurship in the rural areas. Subsidies to co-operative societies do not appear on the execution list of the Ministry of Finance for reasons not difficult to understand.

Price Policies

While the increases in the support/ procurement prices during the last four years have attracted a lot of flak, the fact remains that the rate of inflation in manufactured products stands presently at 11.5% against 5.2% in Food items and average of 8.1%. The terms of trade continue to deteriorate largely on account of state intervention in the agricultural commodity markets.

Administration

The burden of an expensive bureaucracy that is not only corrupt and inefficient, is in fact a handicap for all initiative and enterprise in all sectors. Agriculture as the main incidence-bearer of all indirect taxation is severely affected. Massive slashing of establishment charges, restoration of law and order, reduction in` Law's delays' and re-establishment of sanctity of contract are prerequisites of any serious programme of ER. Since the ER, the situation in this respect has, in fact, deteriorated.

Globalisation in the Indian Context

Globalisation, like Liberalisation, has to be understood in its special Indian context. The autonomy, or rather the insulation of Indian villages from the economy and the polity of the subcontinent has been an age-old phenomenon. It is this isolation that enabled the Country to survive swarms of successive invasions, continuous political turmoil and famines. Villages produced not only food but most of their non-food requirements as well. Few kings dared intervene in the traditional affairs of village panchayats. The farmers, in their turn, were generally indifferent to political changes outside.

Onslaught on Villages

With the coming of the British, the sequestration of villages was ruptured on terms detrimental to agriculture. Goods manufactured in the new factories were thrust on the domestic markets. The village artisans could not withstand the invasion of the mass-produced goods. Even worse, the food requirements of the rapidly expanding urban population were sought to be met through coercive expropriation or uneconomic and skewed trade. Cheap raw material was, after all, the main objective of colonisation. Gandhi's recipe for the plunder of the villages was restoration of the village-autonomy, rather than opening to the global village.

Rural India-Backyard Fiefdom

The Independence came, the trends of the British policy worsened and the 'imperial preference' was replaced by a more restrictive policy of 'Indian preference'. The villages, thus, came to loose in the last 50 years whatever advantage they obtained under the Raj in respect of access to markets and to modern technology.

The urban population and the politicians alike had come to assume rural India as a perpetual backyard fiefdom to be exploited in their interests. The farmers cried in wilderness and their protests fell on deaf ears.

Surprise of Uruguay

Surprise of Uruguay fell on deaf ears. The first reaction of the Indian bourgeois to the news that agriculture was a major topic on the agenda of the Uruguay round of talks was one of disbelief. 'What had agriculture to do with international trade? Exports and imports are affairs of the sophisticated urban businessmen. Farmers produce, whatever they can, to meet the needs of the Country and the rest is acquired by the government from foreign countries as gift or import.' This was the general reaction.

India signed the WTO treaty with certain explicit reservations and some concealed designs. It signed the treaty because it had no alternative. Opening up of the national frontiers and removal of State interventions and trade barriers was the theme of the post-USSR era. India lacked the courage of conviction as also the capacity to go against the tide. The government of India, clearly, was all determined to bypass, circumvent, ignore, procrastinate and thus dodge in every possible way any alteration in the India-Bharat relationship.

Indian Preference: Persecution of the Peasantry

Thus we see that clear stipulations of the WTO treaty notwithstanding, India continues to have a universal PDS, compulsory procurements, levy, restrictions on trade/ transport of primary commodities and dumping in the domestic market of foreign agricultural produce by the government itself.

In the Indian context, liberalization is not so much a process of freeing trade as one of camouflaging persecution of the peasantry. Similarly, globalization does not mean access to the world community but rather marginal softening of the tyrannical system of 'Indian preference'.

The WTO Globalisation

The WTO agreement provides for relaxation of trade barriers at a pace that can only be called innocuous.

The agreement makes the following stipulations for developing countries like India.

- Reduce the Aggregate Measurement of Support (AMS) in excess of 10% by 13.33%
- Reduce the import subsidies by 24% and the quantity of subsidised exports by 14% over a period of 10 years.
- Convert qualitative restrictions on imports into tariffs and then reduce the tariff by 24% over a period of 6 years.
- Provide 3% market access opportunities over a period of 10 years.
- Legislate for the protection of its plant varieties.
- Harmonise the sanitary measures with those in the world community.

These stipulations were intended to reduce governmental interventions in favour of farmers and had little relevance for Indian conditions where farmers are exploited rather than assisted through subsidies.

Aggregate Measure of Support (AMS)

India has the dubious distinction of having imposed on its farming community the world's worst level of negative subsidy. The government has resorted to statistical jugglery to maintain that the AMS (1986-89) in India is minus 18% (correct figure is minus 72%). The Indian delegates smugly and gleefully maintained that India need take no action to reduce the AMS. The literal interpretation of the WTO agreement does not impose any measure for softening the negative subsidies.

As regards tariffs on imports, again the general situation is weird. All countries complain of foreign governments encouraging dumping in foreign markets i.e. selling at prices lower than those in the country of origin. Here in India, the national government itself regularly imports primary commodities like wheat, cotton, sugar etc. even when their landed cost is higher than the prices prevailing in domestic markets.

India has exempted itself from the commitment to provide any minimal access opportunities.

Neo-Colonial Government

Even 4 years after signing the treaty, the legislation relating to Intellectual Property Rights (IPR) and particularly on the protection of plant varieties is in a state of suspended animation is not in place.

India has got extremely high rates of tariffs on imports approved by the WTO. (Edible oil : 300%, processed food :150%, whole commodities :100%). Therefore, it would not be required to take any action for reduction of tariffs on imports of agricultural commodities.

Briefly, the Government of India has taken full measures to ensure that WTO treaty should not alter its neo-colonial relations with Bharat.

Agricultural Exports

Exports of agricultural commodities stood at $3266 million (18% of the total exports) in 1990-91. In 1996-97 it had more than doubled to $6765 million (20.41% of total exports). Marine products ($1123 million), oil-meals ($983 million), non-Basmati rice ($551 million), raw cotton ($453 million) and coffee ($400 million) accounted for almost a half of exports, while cashew nuts, basmati rice, spices, sugar and molasses and tea together represented 25% of the total Indian exports. The traditional Indian dominance in the international tea market is fast eroding; both, Sri Lanka and Kenya have overtaken India.

Exports of Marine products, coffee, spices, rice–basmati, non-basmati and oil-meal have made considerable progress in recent years.

Restrictive Environment

Agricultural exports is veritably the Cinderella story. The much pampered and protected Indian industry is unable to face the international competition while the persecuted agriculture appears more confident. It is a fact universally acknowledged that India continues to be basically a primary producing country and the real hope of improvement in its Balance of Trade situation comes from agricultural rather than industrial exports.

That, agriculture, suffering as it does from massive negative subsidies, denudation of its capital basis and general inadequacy, if not absence, of infrastructural facilities, accounts for 21% of exports as against 28% of the GDP is an heroic story.

The export performance to date gives little indication about the real potential.

Restrictive Export Regime

Most agricultural commodities are subject to very restrictive export regime. Total prohibition, erratic releases of quota, canalization through State Trading Corporation (STC) or NAFED, regulations regarding Minimum Export Price (MEP), complexity of procedures and mulish as well as corrupt bureaucracy would discourage any honest exporter.

Whatever exports take place are in the nature of ethnic or 'cousin to cousin' exports. The sporadic and erratic character of export releases hinders systematic promotion of Indian agricultural produce. Export of mangoes and rice is largely restricted to the requirements of ethnic population abroad.

Export Quota Notifications

The releases of export quota are notified through obscure media (notifications on ministry boards, press insertions that would be understood only by the knowledgeable). The habitués, who are constantly on the prowl, alone get to know of releases and, thus, are in a position to arrange for contracts by telephoning their counter parts abroad–generally, members of their own families. There are few new entrants in the field because of the difficulty in appropriating quotas, obtaining credit and getting through the procedural maze.

Absurd Theories

The restriction on agricultural exports are based on many pseudo-theories. Such as:

1. That export of agricultural produce should be allowed only when there is excess production since exports will result in domestic shortages. Experience over the years belies this dogma. Exports result in better income for the farmers, and hence higher production.
2. That export of value-added products is to be preferred to that of non-value-added commodities. This dogma is insisted upon even in cases where the value-added is less than the cost-added.
3. That food technology is primitive. "Any one can cook a potato chip!" In fact, this is the field where the technology is extremely sophisticated and complex. Farmers have no access to technology that will meet the international standards and tastes. Consequently, Indian agricultural produce is exported brut rather than in the processed form.
4. That export of agricultural commodities is of interest only to the kulaks and offers little to the small farmers. The experience of the grape-exporters has demonstrated that even small and marginal farmers can benefit directly from exports.
5. That a higher rate of exchange for rupee is more desirable because it facilitates cheap imports. A rupee artificially pegged high has been a constant handicap for all export efforts and particularly for farm exports.

Practical Difficulties

The prospects of agricultural exports are rendered bleak because of certain structural defects and deficiencies of the Indian economy and of the agricultural environment

1. A serious practical difficulty arises out of the infrastructural weakness. The farm-gate prices in India mark a substantial comparative advantage. But, by the time the produce is packaged and transported to the port of embarkation most of the advantage gets eroded.
2. The land reforms legislation including tenancy laws and ceiling Acts do not permit cultivation specifically targeted for exports. There is little varietal uniformity and lesser standardization of technology packages. If an enterprising person with modern know-how wishes to enter the field 69
3. The is discouraged by the fact that even a marginal consolidation of fragmented pieces of land is not permitted for more than three years under the land legislation.

4. Indian agriculture is all a small scale affair, quite innocent of large-scale modern organisational structure. 85 to 90% of the international trade is handled by large-scale corporations. India is probably the solitary exception where exports are handled by mini-enterprises.

5. Dependence on erratic monsoons is a perpetual threat that jeopardises regularity of supply and standardization of quality. That is a very serious handicap in export business.

6. Most agricultural inputs are more expensive in India than elsewhere. Fertilizers, agricultural machinery, pesticides, petro-products cost much more in India than abroad. The comparative advantage of Indian produce at the farm-gate is largely due to the cheap rural labour.

7. The uncertainty in government policies regarding exports and imports, absence of forward trading, poor banking infrastructure and the sheer crudeness of the agricultural marketing mechanism result in wide fluctuations in prices. Farmers who are anxious to supply their produce for processing and exports in years of lean prices turn reluctant when the prices are high and soaring.

In order to be suppliers to the world the export products should meet the requirements dictated by habits and tastes of consumers abroad. Today the farmers' access to developed seeds and pesticides is very poor. We are several years behind in the development of seeds and have been a dumping ground for chemical pesticides which are considered out-dated and often are banned abroad.

Prospects for Globalisation

To-date, export of agricultural commodities from India is restricted to about a score of commodities. These traditional export lines can show much better performance if the handicaps enumerated above are removed. Briefly, globalization presupposes a certain minimal level of liberalization and restructuring of the domestic economy.

In recent years, attempts have been made to export fruit, flowers, dried flowers as also semi-perishable and perishable vegetables. In the early years they appeared to give good results, but are facing serious difficulties now. These finer agricultural commodities have to meet very high and rigid standards of size, colour, taste etc. Major-players in the field like Israel, South Africa, Chile are able to meet these standards, thanks to the high level of investment and technology.

International Standards

That level of sophistication would be a distant dream for the Indian producer. He has, nevertheless, been able to enter the global market due to a phenomenon peculiar to agriculture. Even in low capital situation 10 to 20% of the produce can come up to the qualitative exigencies of the foreign markets. Even a tree growing in wilderness may produce some fruit that would meet the international standards. In a situation where capital is scarce and labour cheap, Indian farmer can still hope to export about 10% of his produce.

This marginal export potential can be sustained if, and only if, the remaining 90% can be marketed economically and without hitches in the domestic market. The exporters of grapes, strawberries, in the flush of enthusiasm of export markets, over-looked the need to develop a domestic market and are now ruing the consequences.

Promising New Fields of Export

There are a few virgin fields which show great promise for exports.

1. About 40% of agricultural land in India has not been touched by any chemicals – pesticides or fertilizers. There is a growing demand, particularly in the European countries, for certified bio-food. India could almost lionise this market.

2. A number of Indian herbals and medicinal plants are attracting the inquisitive attention of pharmaceutical giants abroad. Some of these latter have established bases in India with a view to collecting specific plants growing in forests, mountain sides and wilderness. Collecting these plants or undertaking their cultivation offers considerable promise.

3. Rural labour, particularly the female labour have demonstrated a very high degree of in-born dexterity in cross-pollination operations. This should permit India to make a big in-road into the seed-multiplication market.

Conclusion

Villagers in India, the agrarian community have had a long history of insulation which was ruptured only to its disadvantage. The dawn of globalization should permit the birth of the Indian village into an integrated world where the Indian farmer will have a fighting chance despite the long-standing suppression by the State. He enjoys considerable comparative advantage which can be increased by comprehensive liberalization, introduction of modern technology and management and by concentrating investment and enterprise in areas where India enjoys a natural advantages.

Economic Liberalization and Cooperative Entrepreneurship

Economic liberalization connotes "unshackling the economy from deliberating controls and allow the free interplay of market forces to give incentive to enterprises, entrepreneurs and to attract substantial Foreign Investments".

Fundamentally, the Indian government entered into economic liberalization and even now it is considering further liberalization favorably in view of the positive growth and enhanced performance of the Economies of the East Asian countries. They have significantly liberalized their economies in the last two decades, and it is now more than a decade since India adopted a liberalized economic system. The economic liberalization has paved way for the globalization of the economy which means that the Indian economy is fully integrated with the world economy making the whole world become global village but doing global business.

The global system embrace more of capitalist philosophy, rather than socialist philosophy, however the Indian approach shall consider both philosophies in the most favorable manner. The cooperative entrepreneurs shall give credit to Narashinma Rao Government who introduced, "Structural Adjustment Program", which laid down the foundation of globalization in the name of economic reforms and policy adjustment, under this economic policy, several public sector units and semi-public sectors which played a major role in socio-economic development are being destroyed systematically but on the other side, the economic growth rate is increasing (more than 7 percent). Even then, the cooperative sector is being given a raw deal and suffers a great deal due to these policies; several cooperative organizations have been privatized and sold to individuals i.e., the Sugar Cooperative Industries are now being auctioned and sold to the private industrialists.

Growing Social Business in India

"Social entrepreneurship in terms of operation and leadership could be applicable to nonprofit organizations as much as for-profit social enterprises although in terms of activities and legal entity they are very different." Models for social entrepreneurship in India are **Social for-profit enterprise, non-profit** and hybrid **model**, which are discussed in detail in the following sections. In addition to the above-mentioned models, other ways of creating impact in India are through **philanthropy** and through **Corporate Social Responsibility**.

India has been regularly receiving global philanthropic money. Recently there has been a rise in local contributions from wealthy individuals with short and long-term vision. A new breed of high-net-worth individuals from the corporate sector is looking at investing philanthropic money in the form of grants and impact investments. Currently strategic philanthropy in India is still at a nascent stage.

The practice of Corporate Social Responsibility (CSR) in India still remains within the philanthropic space, but has moved from institutional building (educational, research and cultural) to community development. With the communities becoming more active and demanding paired with global influences, CSR is becoming more strategic in nature (i.e. getting linked with business than being philanthropic). By discussing a company's relationship to its stakeholders and integrating CSR into its core operations, the impact needs to go beyond communities and beyond the concept of philanthropy. This opens up big opportunities for the development sector to unlock local capital for not only solving short-term social problems but also investing into long-term social entrepreneurship. With the new Companies Act Bill 2013 every company with either:

- A net worth of INR 500 crore (c.78 milion US$) or
- A turnover of INR 1,000 crore (c.157 milion US$) or
- Net profit of INR 5 crore (c.783'350 US$) needs to spend at least 2% of its average net profit for the immediately preceding three financial years on Corporate Social Responsibility (CSR) activities.

Social Entrepreneurship in India

India is a complex and diverse country that can be considered as big as the continent of Europe. In modern times, India can best be understood in two eras: pre-liberalization India and India post-liberalization (i.e. 1991 onwards). While there is cultural unity in India, there is diversity of seasons and vegetation, histories of people, genetics, features and skin color, cuisine, customs and costumes, language and literature, religions and social attitudes and arts. Each region is distinct and evolved and the communities feel proud of their roots. India has two distinct contexts, namely rural and urban, which are essential in understanding the country.

Since globalization of Indian economy, distinct patterns have emerged in urban metro cities as compared to smaller cities, towns, villages, rural/ low accessible regions in the country. People in Indian tier 1 metro cities (population of +100'000 inhabitants with an increasing middle, upper-middle and upper economic class) can be benchmarked with major global cities across the world.

Socio-Cultural Background

India is among the world's oldest civilization that began about 4'500 years ago. Many sources describe it as "Sa Prathama Sanskrati Vishvavara" — the first and the supreme culture in the world. Early on, Indians made significant advances in architecture (Taj Mahal and many other monuments), mathematics (the invention of zero) and medicine (Ayurveda). Today, India is a very diverse country, with more than 1.25 billion people1, 29 states and seven territories2. Each state is much like a Swiss canton and has its separate state policies, taxation rules and plans aligned with the central (federal) government with the exception of certain subjects such as defense/ military.

Contrary to the popular belief, there is no official language in India. Though many people speak Hindi in India, 59% of India's residents speak something other than Hindi. Bengali, Telugu, Marathi, Tamil and English are also widely used, with approximately 26% of men and 14% of women reported to speak fluent English3. India is identified as the birthplace of Hinduism and Buddhism, the third and fourth largest religions in the world. About 84% of the population identify themselves as Hindu followed by 13% Muslim, making it one of the largest Islamic nations in the world4. Christians, Sikhs, Buddhists and Jains make up a small percentage of the population. India is a secular, democratic republic country under the constitution hosting the world's most diverse communities under one national identity.

Discrimination based on 'caste' is against the law and the government has various programs to ensure equal opportunity, e.g. through quotas. Nevertheless, India is still struggling with the caste system that discriminates among its people, more so in the rural areas where Dalits (Indian name for the lowest caste) and the scheduled tribes still attempt to assert for their rights. The system itself is too complex and is layered through history, across communities, geographies and psychological aspects (upper and lower, forward and backward caste, and sub-casts still prevail). However, these differentiations are dissipating in urban Indian cities.

Economic Background and its Impact

The reforms in 1990s impacted the social, cultural and economic face of urban India with the advent of globalization. Globalization of the Indian Industry opened up its economy for trade, investments, talent and knowledge exchange. Major global companies continue to focus on capturing the imagination of Indian consumers. This brought large amounts of foreign investments into industries such as information technology/ business processing outsourcing (IT/ BPO), pharmaceutical, petroleum, fast moving consumer goods (FMCG) and manufacturing sectors. During this period access to television grew from 20% (1991) to 88% (2012) of the urbAlbiet slow, globalization lead to rural India's progress through commercialization of agriculture and expansion of agro-industries, the liberalization of international trade and an population, with satellite television market penetrating as deep as rural marketing for food and other agricultural products, the intensification and internal labour migration, the increasing privatization of resources and services and the wider use of information, communication and technology.

However, urban India has seen a paradigm shift in lifestyle through communication and consumerism, leading to large numbers of migration from rural to urban areas in search of better job and lifestyle. Urban lifestyle in India is quite different from the rural in terms of cost of living. With growing purchasing powers, there are inequalities in distribution of income/ wealth and resources. Hence, in social entrepreneurship ecosystem, target communities can be categorized as:

- Urban/ rural poor
- Below/ Above Poverty Line (BPL/ APL)

Those spending over INR 32 (c. US$ 0.5) a day in rural areas and INR 47 (c. US$ 0.7) a day in towns and cities are considered APL.

India's service sector is growing exponentially in urban India, attracting the second highest foreign direct investment (FDI) in startups and businesses after China and is estimated to overtake China by 2020. There is a larger push by the government to make India a manufacturing hub for quality products by creating Special Economic Zones (SEZ) and Small/ Medium Industry Corridors across the northern and western parts of the country.

India is with 356 million young people also home to the world's largest youth population (10-24 years old)6 giving a unique opportunity of labor and knowledge skills. However, the challenge lies in providing quality education and skill development to prepare the workforce for a competitive global economy.

Socio-cultural

Hindi and related languages predominate in North India. Hinduism is the main religion while other religions practiced by various ethnic communities include Islam, Sikhism, Jainism and Buddhism. North Indian culture is mainly rooted in Indo-Aryan traditions and customs, with assimilation of and impact from other cultures over long periods of history. North Indian culture reflects the diversity of traditions and customs of the vast region it encompasses.

Economy

The National Capital Region of Delhi has emerged as an economic powerhouse with rapid industrial growth along with adjoining areas of Punjab, Uttar Pradesh, Haryana and Rajasthan. Chandigarh has the highest per-capita State Domestic Product (SDP) of any Indian union territory. New Delhi, apart from being the capital of the country, boasts a large sourcing hub, large industrial/ manufacturing hubs and is known as the unofficial capital for design and creative industry in the country. Chandigarh, Jaipur and Lucknow are now major hubs for business, trade, capital (money) and talent for entrepreneurship apart from Delhi.

Industry

The Northern Region is the largest contributor to the national GDP. Construction, transportation, storage and communication are amongst the fastest growing sectors in the region and are also amongst the top five contributors to the region's GDP. Uttar Pradesh, Rajasthan and Delhi are the three largest economies in the region whereas Chandigarh, Uttarakhand and Haryana are the three fastest growing economies in the region. State-wise best performing sectors include Chandigarh in trade and hospitality, Delhi and Haryana in real estate, Himachal Pradesh in agriculture and Uttarakhand in construction and manufacturing

Social-cultural

In West India, the states of Maharashtra, Gujarat and Goa are culturally varied and distinct. Maharashtrian culture derives from the ancient Hindu Vedic culture influenced deeply by the Maratha Empire. Indian movie industry (Bollywood) has had a huge impact on the lifestyle and culture especially in this part of India, as the industry is primarily located in Mumbai. Gujarati culture is a blend of Indian culture and foreign influence, especially by the Parsis, a community who migrated from Persia to Gujarat about 1000 years ago. Gujarat also saw conquests, as well as a constant stream of migrations from Sindh and Rajasthan that has helped shape the unique cultural landscape of the state. Goan culture, on the other hand is a unique blend of Indian and Portuguese culture, due to its colonial history. The state is very popular amongst tourists, especially for its beaches.

Economy

Mumbai is the most important metro city in Western India followed by Ahmedabad in the state of Gujarat, Pune in the state of Maharashtra and Panjim in the state of Goa. Mumbai as the financial capital of India hosts the headquarters of many large corporations. The city holds a strong historical and economic importance in the country. Pune is fast becoming a major hub with a vibrant startup ecosystem, large academic institutions, young talent, and local capital. Along with this trend, Pune has large multinational companies (MNC) and businesses establishing large manufacturing zones, such as Volkswagen, Mercedes, Tata, ABB, Bombarlier, Burckhardt Compression, Sulzer, Syngenta, General Motors, Maruti Suzuki, etc. Gujarat and its State Domestic Product (SDP) have grown immensely in recent years, hosting large industrial corridors and conducting trade and commerce through their ports. It also hosts major academic institutions.

Industry

Each of the states in West India, with its distinctive niche, potential and capabilities has contributed significantly to the growth story of India. Investors have been observing this region with great interest on account of its abundant natural resources, industrial strengths, sound connectivity, investor friendly ambience and availability of skilled manpower. The region also hosts one of the indomitable stock exchanges - the Bombay Stock Exchange.

It is the hub of some of India's biggest multinationals and world-class tourist destinations. The major manufacturing industries located in the region include basic iron and steel, auto and auto components, engineering, chemical and petrochemicals, gems and jewelry, textiles, agro products, cement and pharmaceuticals, to name a few. In addition, the region also has a robust service sector comprising banking and financial services, legal services, transportation, tourism, entertainment and healthcare.

Social-cultural

The majority of East Indian population is Hindu, with Muslim, Christian, Buddhist and Sikh as minorities. Muslims constitute a very large minority, especially in the state of Bengal (25% of the population) and the state of Bihar (17%). East India has several pilgrimage sites, which attract a steady stream of national and international tourists all year around. The history, migrated people, unique geography, diverse demographics, and its ancient heritage shape the culture in East India. It is a multiethnic society with a vast variety of languages, customs, religions, music, dance and clothing.

Economy

The eastern part of the country, comprising of the states of Bihar, Jharkhand, Assam, West Bengal and Orissa, has largely been a very low contributor to national GDP. West Bengal contributes just about 6% to India's GDP, while the others contribute only 2-3%. This is low compared to the 15% contribution from Maharashtra and 7% contribution from both, Gujarat and Tamil Nadu7. However, things are rapidly changing in the region, especially in and around Kolkata, the capital of the state of West Bengal. Bihar which was considered one of the most backward states in social and economic index has seen a fast growth in SDP (State Domestic Product) with the state government pushing business and entrepreneurship friendly policies and tackling red-tape bureaucracy.

Industry

The eastern region of India is a land of huge potential and is endowed with plenty of rich minerals, forests, productive and fertile soil and rich cultural heritage. Given the available natural resources and quality manpower, the key growth engines are iron and steel, power, mines and minerals, tourism, agro and food processing, infrastructure, IT and ITES, petrochemicals, leather, real estate, retail and cement. The Eastern states have immense potential for large-scale production and export of spices, jute and other agro products.

A spurt in investments coming to these states is an indication of a bright future for trade and industry in the region. There has been a continuous improvement in the hard and soft infrastructure. The growth of IT and ITES, healthcare and tourism in the eastern states coupled with a rapidly developing educational sector unfolds unique advantages adding to the rich intellectual base of the region.

Socio-cultural

The largest linguistic group in South India is the Dravidian family of languages including Telugus, Tamils, Kannadigas and Malayalis. About 80% of South Indians are Hindu, followed by 11% of Muslim and 8% of Christians. Kerala is the state with the highest number of Christians in the Indian Union with over 6 million8. This corresponds to 25% of all Christians in India. The majority of people from South India worship the eternal universe by the means of celebrating the beauty of the body and motherhood through dance, clothing and sculptures. This is also reflected in their way of life.

Economy

The most industrialized cities in South India are Chennai, Bengaluru and Hyderabad followed by Visakhapatnam, Coimbatore, Thiruvananthapuram and Cochin. Chennai is termed as the Gateway of South India, being one of the largest metropolitan cities in India. Bengaluru is the largest southern cosmopolitan city that has now become the startup capital and unofficial entrepreneurship capital of India with capital, talent and resources. This is followed closely by Chennai, Hyderabad and Cochin.

Industry

The southern states, especially Andhra Pradesh, Karnataka, Kerala, Tamil Nadu and Pondicherry have consistently scored high in the country on key economic and social indicators. Tamil Nadu has a strong manufacturing base especially in auto and auto components, Karnataka is globally recognized as the IT hub, Andhra Pradesh's strength lies in biotechnology and pharmaceutical industry, Tourism is an important advantage of Kerala and Pondicherry is becoming one of the key centers for general engineering, auto ancillary and IT/ ITES.

A granular understanding of India's market potential and tailored localization strategies is essential for a success in India. McKinsey's recent study in 20149 has identified key economic and business growth hotspots for the period up to 2025. The study predicts 15 additional metropolitan areas until 2025, after analyzing 29 Indian States and 7 Union Territories in the country. The emerging cities include Jamnagar, Dehradun, Cuttack, Bhavnagar, Kolhapur, Vellore, Amaravati, Ajmer, Udaipur, Sangli, Nanded and Mangalore.

Social innovation helps in solving some of the most pressing problems with new solutions such as fair trade, distance learning, mobile money transfer, restorative justice and zero carbon housing. The process of creating solutions is also profoundly changing beliefs, basic practices, resources and social power structures. Social innovation provides a unique opportunity to step back from a narrow way of thinking about social enterprises, business engagement and philanthropy.

For social innovation in India, a developmental model needs to be designed, keeping in mind the diversity of culture and abundance of its resources, people's aspiration levels and the ecological limitations of nature. Indians are making efforts in creating new avenues for social innovation across sectors, such as education, healthcare, housing, agriculture and livelihoods. There is enough evidence of grass-root innovation amongst the poorest of poor who live with or without any access to technology. These innovations are not only relevant in India but could also be applied globally, highlighting the universal elements of innovation such as ecological sustainability practices, low cost, scalability and optimization of resources. Social innovation segment in India requires support in capacity building and go-to market strategies.

Mr. Subramaniam Ramadorai, adviser to the Prime Minister of India states, that "India needs to unleash technological and social innovations that can usher in a new developmental model the world has not seen before.9a Swiss innovators, funders and universities could look at structured engagement with the Indian social sector by bringing expertise, knowledge and resources to collaborate with the Indian ecosystem which is known globally as a social innovation lab for piloting ideas.

India provides the challenges, constraints, resources and opportunities to create, test and prototype a solution that can have a positive global impact. A successfully tested solution in India can be scaled to many other developing countries.

Education

The education sector in Indian social enterprise ecosystem is one of the largest and most promising sectors for investment. India faces challenges in multiple areas of providing quality education and an all-round development of students who are to become the knowledge and labor power of the economy. The Indian education sector is very big and diverse and can be broadly classified into:

- K-12 education: Kindergarten, Primary & Secondary education
- College and University education: Undergraduate & graduate
- Vocational training

Each category has its own complex challenges and opportunities. This section only discusses the K-12 category that has seen the most severe gaps and poor access to quality education for children. The Indian education sector is one of the largest capitalized spaces in India with an annual Government spend of US$ 63 billion (3.4% of GDP) and an annual private spend of US$ 56 billion. In addition, approximately 200'000 students travel to foreign countries every year and spend about US$ 13 billion on education. This adds up to an annual education spend of US$ 133 billion10. With the largest number of youth population in the world, Indian education sector is highly viable and promising. The sector is beginning to demand larger involvement of social enterprises and requires enhanced Public Private Partnership models (PPP) across the country. Most affordable private schools operate as hybrid for-profit/ non-profit structures in which the school is a not-for-profit entity, but the school management company is a for-profit entity; equity investments take place in the for-profit entity. In contrast to this, the private coaching and education content space is unregulated. The Government's Right for Education (RTE) Act mandates private schools to provide 25%11 of their seats for low-income households with expenses for these seats covered by the government. This policy is facing stiff opposition from school managements, parents, and even those who have stakes in the schools. Social enterprises are working around these challenges through advocacy and capacity enhancing solutions. The private sector, especially social enterprises that deliver services to the BoP play an important role in achieving the RTE mandate.

Another prospective area for growth and investments in the education sector is the preschool segment: with the increasing demonstration effect on the demand for their services, pre-schools are moving to villages as well. However, the engagement of the private sector and growth of social enterprises is hindered by several sector-specific policies and regulatory frameworks. Certain rules still mandate that all formal education institutions operate as not for profit institutions. These regulations restrict equity investment and since formal schools require substantial access to capital this creates constraints for social enterprises.

Challenges

- **High drop out rates:** Nationally 29% of children drop out before completing five years of primary school, and 43% before finishing upper primary school. High school completion is only 42%12. 1.4 million children aged 6-11 in India are not even going to school13.

- **Inadequate school** infrastructure: only 53% of schools have functional girls' toilets14 and 74% have access to drinking water15.

- **Inequality amongst schools:** At the top end are English-language schools affiliated to the upscale CBSE (Central Board of Secondary Education), CISCE (Council for the Indian Schools Certificates Examination) and IB (International Baccalaureate) examination boards, offering globally recognized syllabuses and curricula. Those who cannot afford private schooling attend English-language government-aided schools, affiliated to state-level examination boards that struggle to maintain quality standards and do not focus on an all round development of the child.

- **Teacher shortage:** Teachers are paid low salaries and are not supported with incentives. The Student Teacher Ratio in developed countries stands at 11.4, while in case of India; the ratio on an average is as high as 22.0 leading to teacher absenteeism and large number of teacher vacancies16. There is a teacher shortage of 689`000 teachers in primary schools17.

- **Quality of learning:** The quality of learning in classroom is a major challenge too. Several reports show children are not achieving class-appropriate learning levels. According to Pratham's Annual Status of Education 2013 report, close to 78% of children in Grade 3 and about 50% of children in Grade 5 cannot yet read Grade 2 texts18

- **Affordable private schools:** A number of social enterprises are venturing into affordable private schools, creating a pipeline of budget schools which are well managed and can deliver optimal or basic quality learning environment in K-12 education ecosystem. Partnering and supporting such initiatives at different levels is one of the areas of opportunity for Swiss entrepreneurs.

- **Curriculum development and pedagogy tools:** Technology and other mediums are now actively used to deliver quality-learning material with digital pedagogy tools by social enterprises. There is scope for innovation in creating robust models to provide, monitor and assess the curriculum material provided to schools.

- **Teacher-centric approach:** Teacher training, teaching modules, improved pedagogical tools are some of the areas of intervention for social enterprises.

- **Infrastructure:** This is one of the most untapped areas of opportunity in current K-12 education system. Solutions can range from providing basic hygiene & safe environment such as boundary walls, working clean toilets, safe drinking water to basic furniture, storage and other interior infrastructure for schools.

- **Corporate companies/ CSR:** Majority of corporations in India are investing CSR funds in education as a portfolio. The CSR funds can be invested across various themes and can provide mentorship and other capacity building support to social enterprises in the education sector.

Agriculture

India has primarily been an agrarian economy. Post the industrial reforms in 1990s, Indian economy has witnessed loss of large-scale agricultural lands to deforestation. With automation the agriculture output per hectare has improved but has also led to larger environment degradation. If managed properly, Indian agriculture can not only cater to 1.25 billion people in India but also to many other countries. Agriculture provides livelihood to more than 70% of India's rural population and has a large number of social enterprises, with 44% of enterprises launching in the sector in 2010 or 201119. One-third of agriculture enterprises provide some kind of service to farmers such as teaching organic farming practices. More than 10% of enterprises also offer financial services to low-income clients or producers–primarily access to credit. Yet agriculture enterprises tend to have low penetration across many communities. Agriculture social enterprises can be broadly categorized into:

- Those supporting the value chain pre-harvest with an objective to increase agricultural yield in an economically and environmentally sustainable manner. They are structured as both for-profit and not-for-profit entities. Aakruthi Agricultural Associates and Janani Agriserve20 are two such enterprises. They collectivize small/ marginal farmers, distribute information and advisory services, supply farm equipment, ensure access to quality inputs and teach organic farming practices.

- Those supporting **post-harvest** operations with an objective to eliminate supply chain inefficiencies while ensuring economic profits for all value chain actors. Operations in the post-harvest space require a substantial amount of capital and operational expenditure. Field Fresh Food21, Mother Earth22 and Star Agri23 are 3 such enterprises operating in the post-harvest space. They are actively involved in procurement, storage, transport, processing, and retailing.

- Those that work with the **dairy value chain** engaging in dairy farming, fisheries and allied activities. These social enterprises are structured as for-profit entities and are typically involved in aggregation, procurement, and processing 19.

Challenges

- **Decline in production:** In the name of industrialization, farming land is being taken away from farmers. 80% of farm subsidies go to chemical companies who push chemical fertilizers amongst farmers putting them in huge loans and debts due to crop failures24. There's stagnation and a decline in production, output per hectare in the last three decades.

- **Lack of infrastructure:** Infrastructure and technology support for small scale farmers is lacking. There's a shortage of good quality seeds for poor farmers, inadequate storage facilities and transportation. Lack of efficient water management, soil erosion and better irrigation systems is another big challenge. The techniques and knowhow of organic farming and local ecology is losing significance rapidly, making the farmers totally dependent on external inputs for farming.

- **Decline in interest:** Even though 54.6% of India's population is involved in farming, agriculture sector contributes only 13.9% towards GDP25. The newer generations prefer to migrate to urban areas compared to farming professionally.

- **Decline in land ownership:** Landholding by farmers declined from 2.30ha in the 70s to 1.32 ha in 2000-0126.

- **Lack of support:** More than 250`000 farmers have committed suicide since 199027.

Opportunities

- **Technology:** Swiss innovators can provide access to knowledge, technical insights and mentorship to yield healthy crops and sustainable agriculture practices in India. Swiss innovators can also explore collaborations with grass root level organizations that require capacity building support for small-scale farmers and drought hit areas.

- **Policy influence, sustainable practice advocacy:** Swiss community and researchers can partner and collaborate with relevant international organizations to influence policies at government level in India. Switzerland, which has championed the idea of sustainable practices, can bring strong advocacy tools for Indian social enterprises and non-profits in the agriculture sector.

- **Agricultural mechanization, supply chain, storage design:** Swiss communities can bring their expertise to look at better mechanization products, supply chain system design, efficient storage design and low cost scalable solutions that can make a big difference to poor/ small scale farmers.

- **Post-harvest support:** Swiss entrepreneurs/investors can provide capacity building support for small scale farmers in India to help them build market linkages, eliminate middle-men and tap urban to rural markets for sales.

- **Financial inclusion and support for organic and sustainable framing practices:** Partnering with local organization can help Swiss enterprises to create new models of financial aid and soft loans to allow cooperatives and local farmers to create new business opportunities for themselves

Healthcare

India has a universal public health care system run by the constituent states and territories. Parallel to this public health sector, is the private medical sector in India that is more popular. Both urban and rural Indian households use the private medical sector more frequently than the public sector.

In addition to a health care system, India has several safety net health insurance programs for the high-risk population such as the Community Health Insurance program for the population below poverty line and Life Insurance Company (LIC) policy for senior citizens. All such programs are monitored and controlled by the government-owned General Insurance Corporation. There are additional plans offered to government employees, and a handful of private companies sell private health insurance to the public. Yet many urban and rural poor to middle-class people are not aware of these schemes and programs. India's Maternal Mortality

Ratio (MMR) is estimated high, at 212 per 100'000 live births. India has 48 doctors per 100`000 persons that are fewer than in developed nations28. The availability of doctors is even less in rural areas of India. India has a life expectancy of 64/ 67 years (male/ female)29, and an infant mortality rate of 46 per 1000 live births30. With the World Health Organization's 2000 World Health Report ranking India's healthcare system at 112 out of 190 countries31.

Challenges

- **Rural vs. Urban Divide:** A staggering 70% of the population32 still lives in rural areas with limited access to hospitals and clinics and relies on alternative medicines and government programs in rural health clinics. One such program is the National Urban Health Mission that pays individuals for healthcare premiums which has not been very effective. In contrast, the urban centers have numerous private hospitals and clinics that provide quality healthcare.

- **Need for Effective Payment Mechanisms:** Roughly 70% of patients pay for healthcare out-of-pocket because there are no payment arrangements. According to a newly released report by Swiss Re and Harvard's School of Public Health, 16.7% of Indians were covered by health insurance policies in 201233.

- **Demand for Basic Primary** Healthcare **and Infrastructure:** Basic infrastructure, especially in rural areas is still lacking, with respect to sanitation and water management.

- **Malnutrition:** Dietary risks, protein energy malnutrition, particularly childhood malnutrition continue to be prevalent. 31% of children under 5 are undernourished34 and a third of adult women have a body mass index (BMI) lower than 18.5, a level commonly associated with chronic energy deficiency. The poorest seem to live on less than 1'500 calories a day compared to the norm of over 2'00035.

- **Lack of awareness of mental disorders:** 6-7% of the population is known to have some form of mental disorder36, with no clear distinctions between rural and urban India. Over 90% of mental disorders are also estimated to go untreated37. Many constraints contribute to these gaps, such as cost considerations, socio-cultural beliefs, stigma and overall lackof health literacy

Opportunities

- **Impact Investments:** Healthcare is one of the most sought after sectors for impact investing with funds being channeled into a variety of areas – from hospitals and clinics to innovative diagnostic tools and medical devices designed for low-resource settings. Narayana Hruda-ya-laya38, Arvind Eye Care39 and Embrace Innovations40 are credible organizations that have demonstrated the viability of social enterprises. After hospitals, pharmaceuticals account for the second largest percentage of total funding (13%) given the global success of Indian pharmaceuticals companies in developing low cost generics41Medical devices account for the third largest (again 13% of total investment).

- **Health Insurance:** Nearly 75-80% of Indian population is without a proper health insurance, paying their health care spending out-of-the pocket42.

- **Medical devices:** According to The Economic Times43, the medical devices sector is seen as the most promising area for future development by foreign and regional investors. Recently, the government has been positive on clearing regulatory hurdles related to the import-export of medical devices, and has set a few standards around clinical trials. Swiss quality high tech medical devices, made affordable, can scale rapidly in India.

- **Building centralized information and** raising **awareness:** Improve accessibility to information with offline and on-line Drug Database to improve health delivery system and build local champions for information distribution.

- **Health care infrastructure:** Standardizing diagnostic procedures, building rural clinics, and developing streamlined health IT systems and improving efficiency. 42 Swiss Re: Health Risk Factors India (2015), http://media.cgd.swissre.com/documents/RDS_HealthRisk-   Factors_India_WEB.pdf 43 Economic.

Renewable Energy

India has the fifth largest power generation portfolio worldwide. Coal and gas are the popular sources of energy and account for 58% and 9% respectively of the total energy consumed in the country. India has been rapidly adding capacity over the last few years, with total installed power capacity growing to 223 Giga Watts (GW) in March 2013 from 98 GW in March 1998. Economic growth and increasing prosperity, coupled with factors such as rate of urbanization, rising per capita energy consumption, and a growing middle class are likely to push energy demand further in the country.

The Renewable Energy market is currently valued at US$ 17 billion and growing at an annual rate of 15%. The opportunity lies in the untapped potential in generating energy: only 19.97 GW out of the estimated potential of 200 GW have been utilized thus far44. Demand for power in India has been increasing rapidly due to industrialization and urbanization. The Government of India estimates that the country needs to add 150 GW of power capacity over the next five years - a US$ 200 billion investment coupled with many key incentives are in the pipeline to bridge the supply/ demand gap. There has been a proliferation of social enterprises adopting a variety of business models in the clean energy sector through devices that meet basic lighting and cooking solutions, household energy systems and off-grid energy solutions delivered to large communities. 25% social enterprises surveyed in Intellecap's 2012 Social Enterprise Landscape report45 were dealing with energy and had higher growth compared to other sectors. Given India's share in world energy consumption stands at a meager 4.2% despite being the world's second most populous country, the opportunities to create and increase energy access are very pronounced.

Challenges

- **Lack of** electrification: 280 million people in rural India and 24 million people in urban India are without access to electricity. There will be a scarcity of 467 GW electricity in the next 15 years.
- **Inequality in power supply:** Access to energy and major inequalities in access are major challenges in India. According to the International Energy Agency46, 77 million households in India still use kerosene for lighting.
- **Dilemma with alternate energy sources:** There's a lack of nuclear energy sources to meet the energy demands in India. Renewable energy sources need large investments almost prohibiting the government or public sector units from taking it up. There have been small and large scale hydro-electricity projects approved by states and central government that pose a huge threat to biodiversity of the region, local communities' displacement and loss of livelihoods.

Opportunities

Untapped potential: There is a scope to fullfil the gaps in the following renewable energy sectors:

- Presently, solar only covers 3% of 100 GW potential capacity. Many parts of India receive 300 days of annual sunshine which presents an opportunity for constant solar power generation.
- Only 3% of 4 GW potential capacity is generated through waste
- Only 11% of 18 GW potential capacity is generated through biomass
- Only 19% of 20 GW potential capacity is generated through small hydro

- Presently 53% of 5 GW potential capacity is generated through bagasse cogeneration
- Only 21% of 103 GW potential capacity is generated through wind (onshore)

Delivery models: Social enterprises serve energy-deprived markets in two ways:

- Provide clean energy products (solar lanterns, solar home systems (SHS), solar pumps, solar photovoltaic water heating and energy efficient cook stoves) for efficient lighting and heating/ cooking.

- Provide electricity through micro/ mini grids that use technologies such as biomass-gasify small hydro, solar photovoltaic and wind to supply power to un electrified and under electrified communities. Nuru Energy47, Urja Unlimited48 and Greenway Grameen Infras49, Greenlight Plant50, Urja Unlimited51 and ONergy52 are some notable social enterprises in the energy sector. Swiss startup LED Safari53 has recently begun bridging this gap.

Growth potential and investments: As of 2015 350 GW of offshore wind energy potential is entirely untapped. India's investment target over the next 5 years towards 100 GW solar and 60 GW wind capacity is CHF 100 bilion. SELCO India 54, one of the most credible renewable energy organizations in India has been actively supported and invested by Swiss investors.

Manufacturing

Make in India is an initiative of the Government of India, to encourage companies to manufacture their products in India. It was launched by Prime Minister Narendra Modi on 25 September 2014. In a major boost to the 'Make in India' initiative, the Government has received confirmation from technology firms such as GE, Bosch, Tejas and Panasonic regarding their decision to invest in the electronic, medical, automotive and telecom manufacturing clusters in India. India is an attractive hub for foreign investments in manufacturing sector. Several mobile phone, luxury and automobile brands, among others, have set up or are looking to establish their manufacturing bases in the country. With impetus on developing industrial corridors and smart cities, the government aims to ensure holistic development of the nation. The corridors would further assist in integrating, monitoring and developing a conducive environment for the industrial development.

Industrial manufacturing is a major growth sector for the Indian economy with diverse companies including those engaged in manufacturing of machinery and equipment, electrical and metal products, cement, building and construction material, rubber and plastic products and automation technology products. India needs to create employment of 10 – 15 million jobs per year55 to absorb the growing young population and the service industry cannot meet this demand at scale. Manufacturing industries can contribute as the largest employers to meet this demand.

Challenges

- **Capital-intensive:** Manufacturing is capital-intensive exercise requiring access to loans. High interest rates have been impacting new investments.
- **Lack of domestic demand:** Lack of domestic demand has pushed the manufacturers to look at export markets with the devaluation of Rupee.
- **Shortage of skilled labour:** There is a large shortage of skilled labor for manufacturing and lack of investment in training of skilled labor or improving efficiency. Also the Indian youth prefer white-collar jobs in their search for upward mobility.
- **Global competition:** India is traditionally known for service industry, while a push for large scale manufacturing has only recently begun. There is a tough global competition from established economies, especially China

Opportunities

- **Favorable regulations:** The Interim Budget of 201456 presented by the government of India, proposed changes in indirect taxes to boost manufacturing, including cutting the excise duty on some goods in the capital goods and consumer non-durables sectors such as electrical and construction from 12% to 10%. Manufacturing segments are making investments to enter Tier 2 (50'000 to 99'999 inhabitants) and Tier 3 (20'000 to 49'999 inhabitants) cities in order to boost sales.
- **Fair Trade:** Social responsibility is deeply rooted into Indian culture. Swiss social enterprises in perishable/ non-perishable manufacturing could create or extend fair trade value chains in India.

Skills Development

Skills development as a sector has gained prominence in the social enterprise ecosystem with several skills development and vocational training enterprises rising in the social sector in the last 5 years. Skillsonics India Pvt. Ltd.57 was born with this vision with support from Swiss Federation. This sector is also closely interlinked to the manufacturing sector.

Challenges

- **Employability:** Number of young university graduates is rapidly increasing every year, and the industry is not sufficiently hiring these fresh graduates, leaving large numbers of individuals either unemployed or wanting skills training and development. In addition, the development of information and communication technology (ICT) is occurring at unprecedented speed, requiring workers to have more, and more complex, cognitive skills.

- **Lack of skill and training:** With 12.8 million young people newly entering the labor market very year58, the government recognizes that the country faces a serious skills shortage, as the majority of these new labor market entrants are likely to remain unskilled.

- **No access to skill training:** Despite India's projected demographic dividend and its abundant labor supply; it suffers from a serious shortage of skilled workers, because of their limited access to education and skills training and large skills mismatch in the labor market.

- **Social stigma:** The demand for vocational training has generally been low even among the socially disadvantaged. Students prefer white-collar jobs in their search for upward mobility. Vocational training has largely been seen as a second-choice option for economically disadvantaged and/or academically less capable.

- **Lack of interest in skill training:** Most of the skills training institutes are set up in rural or a semi-urban area where ensuring steady flow of enrollments and an acceptable level of capacity utilization is a constant challenge for training providers

Opportunities

- **Demand for vocational/ skill training:** By 2025, India will have a working population (age 15-64 years) of approximately 959 million people59 and most of them will require vocational/ skill training.

- **National focus on skills development:** Recently, India set up Prime Minister's National Skills Development Council (NSDC) to coordinate various schemes provided by various ministries. Switzerland's expertise on vocational education and skills development is very well known and appreciated across India.

- **Advisory for skill councils:** Swiss experts and institutes could advise existing social enterprises and non-profits in India for developing policies, setting priorities and strategies and overseeing and coordinating the various stakeholder initiatives and efforts.

- **In-firm skills training:** Only 17% of manufacturing firms in India provide any training for employees60. High growth areas such as manufacturing, automotive, retail, trade, transport, construction, hospitality and healthcare have the ability to provide the required expanded employment. Public private partnerships in the country are already in the process of strengthening rural infrastructure such as Industrial Training Institutes (ITIs), polytechnics, community polytechnics and vocational education in secondary schools. Workers such as technicians, welders, fitters, paramedics, tourist guides etc. are to be skilled with a twofold objective- first, to close the skill gap of an already qualified workforce and second, to provide formal vocational training to those who have acquired skills informally.

Diversity

India is a very heterogeneous society, with 29 states, 7 union territories, 23 recognized languages, rich culture, numerous sub-groups, ethics, and religious believes. It is important for Swiss social enterpreneurs seeking growth opportunities in India to fully appreciate the diversity and layers of India and to have a long-term vision, which requires time and patience.

Cultural Differences

Indian culture is clearly different from the European. The general national tendencies can be identified, especially when comparing with a western country, such as Switzerland. The following five themes capture these tendencies61.

Power Distance/ Importance of Hierarchical Position

Indian society has a strong appreciation for hierarchy and a top-down structure in society and organizations. It is common, that the boss takes most of the decisions and the employees execute. Power is mainly centralized and managers count on the obedience other team members Employees normally expect to receive clear tasks and processes are divided into many individual tasks, each of them being executed by another person. This is in contrast to Swiss business culture which tends to be of flat hierarchy. Business communication in India is top down and directive in style, with mostly no negative feedback given towards someone up the hierarchical ladder

Individualism vs Collectivism

India can be seen as both individualistic as well as collectivistic. There is a high preference to belong to a larger social framework where individuals are expected to act according to the greater good of one's „in-group". In these situations, the opinion of one's family, extended relatives, neighbours, work group and other wider social networks influence the actions of the individual.

The relationship between employer and employee is based on mutual expectations –loyalty by the employee and almost familiar protection by the employer. Hiring and promotion decisions are often made based on relationships

Masculinity vs. Femininity

In a masculine society, people seek to be the best and stand out, whereas people in a feminine society are much more motivated by doing a work which they like. In India success and power is often visually displayed. However, India is also a very spiritual country with millions of deities and religious philosophies. Being an ancient country with one of the longest surviving cultures, value of humility and abstinence are also part of Indian culture. Switzerland is ranked as more masculine compared to India, with a strong focus on success and achievements, validated by material gains. Work is seen as the center of one's life.

Uncertainty Avoidance

Especially in comparison to Switzerland, India has a much higher tolerance towards imperfection and uncertainty. Rules are seen as possibilities to circumvent and people rely on innovative methods to "bypass the system". A word often used in India is "to adjust", which means finding an unique and inventive solution to a seemingly insurmountable problem. This attitude is both the cause for misery as well as the most empowering aspect of the country. There is a saying, that, "nothing is impossible" in India, as long as one knows how to adjust.

Long Term Orientation vs. Short Term Orientation

In India the concept of "Karma" influences religious and philosophical thought. Time is less important as in western country, and is not seen as linear. A lack of punctuality is often forgiven, as well as a changing game-plan based on changing reality and a general comfort with discovering the fated path as one goes along rather that playing to an exact plan.

Local Processes and Routines

Local routines and processes differ strongly from Switzerland. A good network and the help of local experts is therefore required. Swiss entrepreneurs should immerse themselves in the local ecosystem by working from public spaces, using public transportation and visiting the same places as their local colleagues. The exposure to the local populations daily situations and difficulties enables a better understanding of customers' needs.

Finding the Right People & Building a Network

Building the right team is a challenge in every country. India differs in the sense, that a lot is based on referrals and your own opinion. You need to spend time to build your network in order to differ honest referrals from others. It is essential to find the right people through research and networking at the right venues. Relationships are key to everything in a Collectivistic society

Underestimating the Existing Ecosystem

India has one of the most sophisticated social entrepreneurship ecosystems, with a long history of civil struggle. The challenge lies in the exploration of the countless movements in this sector and understanding the already existing ecosystem. It is important to come as much with a mind to learn, and not just with a mind to give. Opportunities for social entrepreneurs in India are countless. Overall it can be said, that the huge number of people, the low cost levels, the vibrant social enterprise ecosystem and India's challenges with poverty are main reasons for Swiss social stakeholders to focus on the Indian market.

Out of India's current population of 1.3 billion people, 55 percent are deprived, suffering a severe and damaging lack of basic material and cultural benefits. 67.6% live in rural areas, with agriculture being their major occupation62. India's population is the world's second largest after China and still increasing by 1.25% per year.

Effects of this rapid population growth are:

- Providing employment to growing population
- Problem of utilisation of manpower
- Over-strained infrastructure
- Pressure on land and other renewable natural resources
- Increased cost production
- Inequitable distribution of income63

These effects offer countless opportunities for Swiss social stakeholders to bring innovative solutions to the Indian market. India is one of the cheaper countries, based on data from the OECD Consumer Price Index64. Compared to the costs of Switzerland as well as other countries of the global south, India offers the opportunity to launch a business with a relatively low amount of investment (see chapter 10. Cost of launching in India for more details).

Another opportunity lies in India's vibrant social enterprise ecosystem, which is the most elaborated ecosystem worldwide and consists of:

- An openness to market-driven approaches
- Foreign capital that sees jugaad-driven entrepreneurism in India as the future
- India's new rich who are beginning to explore alternative philanthropy
- The multitude of domestic social impact funds that have supported the ecosystem for the last decade and
- The Indian government, that has funded numerous social initiatives65.

Mr. Klaus Schwab, Founder of the World Economic Forum and the Schwab Foundation states, that "India has some of the most advanced and innovative social entrepreneurs. We believe and already see that many of the models developed in India, for instance rainwater harvesting for schools pioneered by Barefoot College, are exported around the world. India is therefore a key country to look for leading social entrepreneurs."65a In addition to the opportunities mentioned, there are specific arguments for each group of stakeholder.

Swiss Entrepreneurs

India, being a country with some challenges, offers at the same time endless opportunities to tackle and provide a solution for each one of them. Swiss entrepreneurs can use their sector specific expertise and strengths, especially in the fields of vocational education, healthcare and renewable energy. By establishing collaborations and partnerships with local organizations, Swiss entrepreneurs could share their expertise and learn about sociocultural context. In India, numerous opportunities lie in low-tech approaches, with low-need for maintenance and locally sourced components, making it affordable. Swiss entrepreneurs can use India as a market with low entry costs to build and test prototypes with innovative ideas, gather feedback from different and diverse communities and scale the successfully tested solution across the world.

Swiss Impact Investors

Capital investment into impact enterprises is still relatively low in India. However, a fast change and rapid increase can be seen (from a trickle of US$ 1.17 million in 2000 to investments of about US$ 250 million per year since 201166), especially due to India's numerous impact entrepreneurs, who received widespread international interest for the replicability of their innovations across emerging markets. Since the early 2000s, more than 50 impact funds67 have emerged in India. Nevertheless the access to capital is the biggest challenge for social enterprises, which increases the importance of impact investors as source of finance.

The potential for Swiss impact investors is remarkable, as domestic capital remains exclusive. In addition, India's impact funds have a sharp focus on scalable business models. This creates a huge gap in availability of capital for impact enterprises which can create deep impact but may not be highly scalable.

Swiss Institutions

India offers unique exploration and education opportunities for international students in the social sector. Dedicating time and resources in research and development, prototyping and innovating in the Indian social sector could be very rewarding. Swiss federal institutes, summer schools and social enterprises could collaborate with the Indian social sector for early exposure of their students to a vast and diverse action field for social solutions. Students can find credible research and experimentation as India is the biggest social innovation lab for the world. Swiss talent can learn in India more easily than other countries such as China, due to language, evolved start up ecosystem and a democracy which creates more transparency. In addition, India is increasingly becoming an important entity in the global market and it is important for younger generations to understand and appreciate the opportunities that India presents.

Swiss Businesses

India is an attractive market for Swiss Businesses, being one of the emerging and fast growing economies. Since 2013, companies of a certain size are obliged to spend a defined amount of their revenues on Corporate Social Responsibility (Companies Act)68. This law led to an increase in CSR spending as well as to a stronger scrutiny of company behavior by Indian society.

Good CSR practices can bring greater benefits, some of which are as follows:

- In India, the community as a stakeholder becomes increasingly important, and the 'license to operate' is no longer given by governments alone, but the communities that are impacted by a company's business operations. Thus, a robust CSR programme benefits both the community and the company, receiving the support of the community and precluding the 'trust deficit'.
- Strong CSR commitments enable the company to attract, retain and motivate employees in India. It increases employee morale and identification towards the company.

- Communities as suppliers: There are certain innovative CSR initiatives emerging, wherein companies have invested in enhancing community livelihood by incorporating them into their supply chain. This has benefitted communities and increased their income levels, while providing these companies with an additional and secure supply chain. Internship opportunities could be supported by Swiss Businesses, in order for young Swiss talent to get exposure to the challenges in India, its culture and characteristics. This could be part of the company's CSR strategy. Regarding the already existing vibrant Indian social impact ecosystem, the number of qualitative ideas is high and so are the opportunities to fund such innovation driven projects.

India's social entrepreneurship ecosystem is reflective of the diversity in regions, its people, unique local challenges and opportunities. At a bird's eye view, a triangular ecosystem is emerging amongst three metro cities, namely: Delhi, Mumbai and Bangalore. However, a host of other prominent social sector organizations across regions engage, influence and thrive amongst India's social entrepreneurship ecosystem.

The Indian social entrepreneurship ecosystem exists at three levels:

1. Urban cities
2. Regional: specific rural and semi-urban areas of a specific region/ state.
3. National: spread across geographies with specific target communities in rural or/ and urban areas.

Funds

Indian social entrepreneurship ecosystem consists of diverse impact investors who engage at different stages of social enterprises:

- **Seed** Fund/ **Seed stage:** Example – Unitus Seed Fund69, the largest seed fund for social enterprises in India.
- **Series A funding/** Growth **stage:** Example – Aavishkaar Fund70, Indian Angel Network71, Grassroots business fund72, LGT Venture Philanthropy73, VenturEast74.
- **Series B funding/ Scale Stage:** Example: Acumen Fund75, Elevar Equity76, Aavishkaar Fund77, Omnivore Partners78, Khosla Ventures79.
- The entrepreneurs in India are no longer only looking at funds or investors for capital or access to network but also for in-depth mentorship and capacity building support. While present day funds/ investors are not just looking at funding or guiding an entrepreneur, but at a deeper level of engagement and commitment to portfolio

companies in helping them grow. Indian social sector is perhaps the second largest pool of concentrated investors after the tech sector.

Incubators/ Accelerators

There are very few incubators/ accelerators in India exclusively focused on social enterprises, however, there are few commercial incubators/ accelerators who have taken up incubation of enterprises that are not only strong on revenue and scale but also have measurable social impact. Incubators/ accelerators offer the following services in combination and not necessarily all services due to limited resources depending on their respective focus, resource availability, access to capital and so on:

- Mentorship
- Co-working space
- Seed fund
- Non-core services
- Networking/ events
- Trainings/ workshops

Two national scale broad approaches have been observed. One kind of incubator looks at focusing on local/city/regional impact helping local entrepreneurs to focus on solving local challenges/problems. The incubator's overall focus is on the idea stage and on early stage of a company where failure/risks are high. The second type of incubator looks at intervention at three different levels across India (1. local inspiration, 2. workshops/ events, 3. incubator/ accelerator) that can lead to more quality enterprises incubated and overall activation of the ecosystem. Support at various stages of incubation:

- **Idea/ seed stage incubation:** Presently, social incubator UnltdIndia80 provides support to idea stage social entrepreneurs that are looking to develop and pilot their social impact ideas, by providing capacity support, mentorship and small capital to help them get-off the ground.

- **Early stage incubation:** Villgro81 based in Chennai is a comprehensive social incubator providing seed fund, mentorship; working **space** and network to social enterprises. It is also working on building active ecosystems in metro and tier 2 and 3 cities by conducting workshops, offering fellowships and organizing mentorship/ networking events.

- **Accelerator:** Villgro also has an **accelerator** program. There are mainstream accelerators and programs that support startups and a small percentage (2-5%) of social enterprises.

Network & Communities

Online Platforms

There are online communities and platforms that promote, support and engage with the social enterprise ecosystem. Online community such as Your Story82 is a media platform that promotes and publishes social sector stories. Ennovent83 is an online platform that supports social enterprises across the country with mentorship, network, events and connections for funding. Start-up Wave84 is an online incubator for social enterprises currently at a pilot stage funded by GIZ85 and managed by Intellecap86 India.

Forums/ Networks

India now sees active forums to discuss, share, network and engage the social enterprise ecosystem more closely and explore possible opportunities. The forums and network are generally large in scale and there are smaller forums that are region/ local ecosystem focused. This also allows organizations to share current updates, opportunities and challenges across sectors and geographies. Sankalp Forum87 is the largest social sector gathering in Asia and has a presence in Africa.

The event hosts organizations across sectors representing social enterprise ecosystem and supports social entrepreneurs through its parent organizations - Intellecap and Aavishkaar Fund88. National Entrepreneurship Network (NEN)89 supports student entrepreneurship across colleges & institutions in India and has actively engaged the academic institutions and state government.

Co-Working Spaces/ Innovation Driven Spaces

The co-working culture in India is brimming. Bangalore witnesses a co-working space every few kilometers. There are spaces such as Bombay Connect90, 91 Springboard Ventures91, Jaaga92 and Bangalore Alpha Lab93 that also organize events, workshops and programs which facilitate sharing and learning for entrepreneurs within a space/ open community.

India also has spaces, events, and competitions which actively promote innovation and social entrepreneurship. To name a few, there are NASSCOM 1000094 startups (includes social enterprises), B-Pac95 (a collective that offers civic governance and citizen engagement programs), Jaaga96 (art and technology driven innovation space), Good Impact Challenge, Mahindra Rise challenge97.

There is a rise in "maker spaces" across the country to prototype deas (such as Workbench projects in Bangalore98) that allows social enterprises to prototype products/ services.

Corporate Sector/ CSR

In the impact sector, generally the corporate have foundations or trusts that are company initiated but independent in operation and objective. The CSR initiative is closely linked to company's mandates.

Recently there has been an upsurge in CSR activities with emphasis on measuring impact, defining clear short and long term goals and importantly adopting models of 'reporting' the social impact made through the initiatives.

In general, corporate CSR and corporate linked foundations have followed three general approaches to engage with the government and the social sector:

1. Integrate with the sector and work closely with the state government.
2. Collaborate with sectors or the government for specific goals or projects. Part ownership allows the corporate to manage diverse projects, measure impact, and then hand over effectively to partner organizations in the social sector or government departments.
3. Independent from government or social sector, implying conceptualization and execution of independent initiatives. Enabling the company to manage projects more effectively, experiment with independent/alternative ideas and models of social impact.

The common challenges with CSR are:

- CSR is still seen through the lens of marketing initiative by majority of companies
- CSR still needs to show tangible outcomes of social impact
- Many MNCs that have a large India presence do not have an India specific CSR policy. The CSR policies are not de-centralized and mandated by the global headquarter. These initiatives lack local context in design and execution

Institutions

Traditional academic institutes have incubated and supported students with labs for R&D, innovation and prototyping. Riding on the big wave of entrepreneurship, institutes have created incubators across themes and sectors such as Indian Institute of Technology (IIT) Bombay99, Chennai100, Indian Institute of Management (IIM)101, National institute of Design (NID)102, Indian School of business (ISB)103.

India now hosts more than 80 student incubators in academic institutes in the area of innovation, technology, manufacturing and entrepreneurship. Research institutions are also on the rise that focuses on specific thematic and sectoral practices offering academic courses, innovation research labs, think-tanks, policy research and network partnering with various non-profit organizations, social enterprises, government, corporate and other ecosystem players. For example, Indian Institute for Human Settlement (IIHS) 104 focuses on urban city challenges in India.

Tata Institute for Social Sciences (TISS)105, Institute of Rural Management Anand (IRMA)106 and Azim Premji University107 are active contributors to the social enterprise ecosystem offering quality academic courses, research opportunities and labs. Graduates get hired in the social sector quite well or move on to build their own social enterprises There are a number of reasons and implications of choosing the right legal structure, such as, how the social enterprise gets funded, how the profits (if any) get distributed, governance structure, reporting responsibilities, tax liabilities, and ownership pattern. India, unlike many other countries – like the US and the UK – does not have plenty of leeway in terms of legally structuring a social enterprise. India has the following three types of legal structures that social enterprise can opt for108:

Non-Profit or Public Charitable Organization

A non-profit is legally structured in India as a charitable Trust (under the Indian Trusts Act, 1882), NGO (under of the Companies Act, 1956) or Society (pertaining to societies registration, of the concerned state). The non-profit has to use approximately 80% of its funds as charity for public good and 20% of its funds for operational and internal organization costs. Non-profits work on grants model but they can earn revenue that has to be for 100% charity in fund usage.

The biggest benefit of registering, as a non-profit is the eligibility to get tax benefits under the Income Tax Act of 1961 and they can also accept foreign donations under the Foreign Contribution (Regulation) Act. One of the problems with this model is that perhaps the inability to hire top-class talent or invest in latest technology and infrastructure. Pros: Ability to focus solely on creating social impact without the pressure of financial return. Cons: Constant needs to raise funds.

The For-Profit Social Enterprise

Social enterprise is legally structured as a for-profit/ business entity with a clear social impact goal defined. In India, there are five options to setup up a for-profit social enterprise: Sole proprietorship, partnership, limited liability partnership, private firm and as a co-operative. 80% of Indian social enterprises are structured as a for-profit private limited company (PLCs)109 . This type of legal structure is perhaps best suited for social enterprises that are looking for growth and profitability. The business model is based on the social impact it wants to make or the social problem it is trying to solve. Key features of social enterprise are:

- The benefactors of the impact and target customers paying for the product or service might or might not be the same.

- The enterprise can be structured for impact investments with options of debt or equity; will report its profits or returns as well as its social impact reporting of their work.

- The social enterprise internally functions like any other commercial business in terms of management, operations, people and resources.

  Pros: Ability to attract funding from VCs, pay top dollar for good talent and invest in technology and infrastructure.

  Cons: Sometimes focus on profits leads to mission drift that makes the original shareholders and stakeholders unhappy.

The Hybrid Model

With the evolution of the concept of social entrepreneurship, new successful models of sustainable income have been seen. The hybrid model brings a non-profit entity and a business (for-profit) entity together to solve the social problem. The non-profit entity is able to raise/ accept grants for the benefactors and at the same time, it can charge for its services/ products through its business entity as a revenue model. The hybrid model helps organizations aiming to achieve high social impact by offering them cross subsidy options that strike a balance between customer acquisition and quality access of services to benefactors.

Pros: This is the best of both worlds, allowing a social enterprise to separate the social and revenue generating activities. The model ensures, that social enterprises can both attract donations and grants, and still be able to have access to social venture funding.

Cons: Focusing on both types of entities could be a problem and so the issue of building a common culture. The report highlights the challenges and opportunities for social innovation in India with respect to education, agriculture, healthcare, renewable energy, manufacturing and skills development. It is advisable for startups and other social impact stakeholders from Switzerland to learn the Indian way of conducting business and understanding the Indian market, rather than imposing global business models and practices.

As the social challenges, which India is facing, are numerous, it has presented a vast range of opportunities for entrepreneurs and startup companies to grow in India. Collaborations between Swiss and Indian social entrepreneurship ecosystems could be established in order for both sides to benefit from each other.

- Swiss entrepreneurs could use their sector specific expertise and strenghts in India and in return learn from the biggest social innovation lab in the world.
- Swiss impact investors can take advantage of India's untapped market with a huge potential for strategic financial intervention.
- Swiss Institutions could collaborate with the Indian social sector for early exposure of their students to a vast and diverse action field for social solutions.
- Swiss Businesses could engage directly with the Indian social sector through strategic Corporate Social Responsibiliy intiatives in order to have a social impact and to strenghen their brand in the world's second largest consumer market. The challenges which are discussed in the report remain. swissnex India, together with a wide network of Social Enterprises, Incubators, Funds, Accelerators, foundations, etc. provide support in order for the Swiss social stakeholder to successfully enter the Indian market. Overall, India is a vibrant place with tremendous opportunities to have an impact.

Role of Government and Policy for Social Enterprises in India

There is increasing recognition within India's central and state governments about the usefulness of engaging or facilitating the private sector to address some of the country's pressing developmental needs, although the specific nomenclature of "social enterprises" is not often used. The Government has been involved in three main categories: Micro, Small, and Medium Enterprises (MSMEs) engagement, government-backed venture capital funds, and policy formulation. First, the government has initiated various public–private partnerships in key development sectors, such as health. For example, many state governments have invited private sector players to provide emergency health care services in urban areas. MSMEs have been identified as a priority lending sector. This increases the availability of capital through government provisioning of grants, equity, and subsidized loans for companies in this category. This clustering includes all enterprises with an initial outlay below $2 million. Since almost all for-profit SEs fall into this category, they will benefit from this policy. Recently, the Prime Minister of India also commissioned a special task force to provide a set of recommendations on further developing India's MSMEs. The task force recommended that the government should spend around $1.1 billion over the next 3 to 5 years on augmenting infrastructure and technological support for MSMEs; of these funds, around 20% should be earmarked for incubation centers within reputable educational institutions.

Secondly, the National Innovation Council, set up by the Prime Minister in 2010 to catalyze innovation in India, is considering establishment of a government-backed venture capital fund. The size of this fund will be in the ballpark of $200 million. The primary focus of this fund would be to address developmental needs in education, health, infrastructure, and sanitation.

Thirdly, the government is involved in formulating and changing policies and regulations that can affect the SE space. Most recently, the Securities and Exchange Board of India (SEBI), the country's financial market regulator, floated a policy paper suggesting the need to separately recognize and regulate "Social Venture Funds". It outlined that these funds are for investors seeking "muted" returns in their investments in return for social gains. SEBI sought public comments on its note and the final recommendations are yet to be finalized.

Different Types of Social Enterprise Models and How They Raise Funds

Social Enterprises have adopted innovative business models with for-profit entities account for three-fifths of all SEs. For-profit models also include collective ownership structures such as cooperatives and producer companies; Waste Ventures is one such organization that "incubates solid waste management companies owned and operated by waste pickers."

About one-fifth of SEs adopt not-for-profit structures, such as Aravind Eye Care Hospitals, which is registered as a trust, and sustained by charging users for affordable eye care. About 20% of the models can be categorized as hybrid, wherein two or more entities, while not legally bound, work in close synergy with each other, usually because they are both founded by the same individual or individuals. The Cash for Group, which comprises both for-profit and not-for-profit entities, is a prime example of this. A growing trend observed in the Indian SE space is the transformation of many not-for-profit models into for-profit models, as these are in a better position to secure financing and scale over time. This was especially true of non-profits in microfinance, where the revenue model was clear early on. Many leading microfinance institutions (MFIs), such as SKS and Spandana, were registered initially as non-profits and subsequently transformed into for-profit companies.

An initial assessment of the SE financing landscape indicates that the key sources of capital for SEs are non-institutional debt, equity (mostly self-finance), institutional debt, and The key sources of equity in the SE space are early stage impact investors or entrepreneurs' capital (both equity and debt). Traditional private equity investments in SEs are rare, and are largely limited to the more developed sectors such as microfinance, health, and agribusiness. This is primarily due to the fact that the markets are developing, business models are just starting to show proof of concept, transaction costs are high for investors, and there is limited data available to help understand the space

Key Social Enterprise Sectors

Affordable Healthcare

Poor households in India spend approximately $6.2 billion annually on healthcare services; in-patient care and pharmacy drugs account for 30% and 33% of the total healthcare expenditure, respectively. The primary reason for such high expenditure by the poor is inadequate public healthcare infrastructure and poor access to existing facilities. Given the potential demand, there is an immense need for healthcare enterprises that provide affordable and quality primary, secondary, and tertiary medical services.

Social Enterprise Involvement in the Sector

The affordable healthcare sector in India is still nascent. The average size of enterprises by revenue is approximately $1.1–$2.2 million. In order to address the market need, affordable healthcare providers use innovative operating models such as leased premises and hub-and-spoke setups in order to minimize the cost of service delivery across primary, secondary, and tertiary care. In the past, affordable healthcare initiatives were largely structured as charitable institutions run by large industrial houses or government operated institutions. With the recent wave of entrepreneurial activity in affordable healthcare, most new initiatives are structured as for profit enterprises. Because affordable healthcare initiatives are young and utilize innovative operating models, many have yet to prove their financial viability. The flow of equity capital has thus been limited to micro-venture capital, with few private equity transactions. The flow of equity to the sector is approximately $118 million with an average deal size of less than $5 million. However, the flow of equity capital to enterprises in affordable healthcare is expected to increase over the next few years as the sector is exhibiting immense growth and first movers are expected to breakeven in the near future. Given the untapped market potential in tier-two and -three cities, the affordable healthcare market is expected to growth rapidly over the next few years.

Policy Enablers and Barriers

The Government generally encourages enterprises in affordable healthcare. For instance, publicly funded healthcare micro-insurance initiatives, such as Rashtriya Swasthya and Bima Yojana, create an incentive for enterprises to deliver healthcare to the poor. However, licensing requirements for all hospitals are cumbersome; hospitals require about 18 licenses prior to commencing operations.

Overview and Need Assessment

The formal real estate and housing finance markets traditionally cater to middle and high income customers, while the government is generally expected to serve the housing needs of the poor. Despite several government initiatives, there exists a huge gap in the supply of affordable housing. The gap in the urban housing market is estimated at 25 million units, virtually all of which is accounted for by the working poor. The estimated gap in the urban housing translates into a market potential of approximately $280 billion.

SE Involvement in the Housing Sector

Given the initial success of housing for low income populations and the potential demand, the market witnessed the entry of specialized enterprises that focused on affordable housing projects and affordable housing finance. Today, India has more than 25 developers involved in affordable housing projects that offer apartments in the price range of $6,600–$15,500.

In affordable housing projects, developers create economic value by minimizing construction cost and time to completion through integrative technical solutions and process innovations. Despite the immense potential demand, the key challenge in developing affordable projects is the unavailability of land close to business districts. The location of an affordable project has an impact on the uptake of housing units, which consequently affects the financial viability of the project. Similar to traditional real estate projects, affordable housing projects are funded through a combination of equity, debt, and pre-construction finance by potential buyers. Although the flow of equity to the sector is gradually increasing, debt continues to be a key source of finance for housing projects. The other key stakeholders in the affordable housing space are the micro-housing finance companies that address the consumer finance needs. The key challenges to serving the micro-housing finance market are lack of consumer credit history and absence of asset collateral. Housing finance companies mitigate the credit risk through stringent project screening and collateralizing the purchased housing unit.

Policy Enablers and Barriers

In order to address the gap in housing supply, the government has instituted various incentive schemes like slum re-development initiatives that attract private capital. However, in order to make affordable housing projects financially attractive, the government will need to provide additional benefits such as tax incentives for developers. The housing finance companies are structured as Non-banking Financial Companies (NBFCs) and have access to wholesale debt funds from commercial banks and the National Housing Bank (apex body in housing finance operated by the Reserve Bank of India).

Agriculture

Overview and Need Assessment

Agriculture and allied sectors provide livelihoods to more than 70% of the rural population in India. Despite this, agriculture accounted for just 14.6% of GDP in 2009–10 as compared to 17.8% in 2007–08.The decline in growth of agriculture and allied sectors is a result of multiple factors, including small farm holdings, poor access to credit, dependency on monsoons, lack of adequate capital investments, poor knowledge of modern agricultural practices, misaligned government policies, and other institutional inefficiencies.

Social Enterprises Involvement in the Agriculture Sector

Social enterprises that operate in the agriculture space create economic and social value by eliminating inefficiencies that exist in the current value chains. These enterprises can be broadly categorized into those supporting the value chain pre-harvest, those supporting post-harvest operations, and those that work with the dairy value chain. The products and services offered by SEs operating in the pre-harvest category attempt to increase agricultural yield in an economically and environmentally sustainable manner. Aakruti Agricultural Associates and Janani Foods are examples of SEs in this category. These SEs collectivize small/marginal farmers, distribute information and advisory services, supply farm equipment, ensure access to quality inputs, and teach organic farming practices. The business models of enterprises operating in the pre-harvest space vary based on products or service offered and legal structure. These enterprises are structured as both for-profit and not-for-profit entities. Enterprises in the post-harvest space attempt to eliminate supply chain inefficiencies while ensuring economic profits for all value chain actors. Field Fresh Food, Mother Earth, and Star Agri are Social Enterprises operating in the post-harvest space. SEs in this space are actively involved in procurement, storage, transport, processing, and retailing. Operations in the post-harvest space require a substantial amount of capital and operational expenditure, causing most business models to be structured as for-profit entities. Dairy farming is a growing activity for SEs in the agricultural space. These SEs are typically involved in aggregation, procurement, and processing and are structured as for-profit entities. Many for profit dairy enterprises also have substantial farmer ownership. Those that are focused on capacity building and training of the dairy farmers are typically structured as not-for-profits. Despite attractive business economics, the dairy farming sector is in its early stages of development and has not attracted significant investor interest.

Policy Enablers and Barriers

The government has instituted several schemes, such as a capital subsidy scheme, to promote investment in the post-harvest space. One of the key challenges facing SEs operating in the post-harvest space is the high level of market regulation, especially in the procurement and pricing of agricultural commodities. The flow of equity capital to the sector is limited to micro-venture capital and impact investments. However, mature companies in the organic agriculture space, such as Suminter Organics, are able to attract substantial investor interest. Recently, a new legal form, "producer company" was instituted to promote for-profit models aggregating producers. Indian Organic Farmers and Vanilla India are two recently formed producer companies. However, the response to the new legal structure has been limited as the structure is not flexible enough to accept external equity, thus limiting growth through external equity. Many agri-businesses thus register as a private limited company instead as this allows them to raise capital, though this limits the potential social impact because of lack of farmer-based ownership in the company.

Education

Overview and Need Assessment

The education sector In India lacks the capacity to educate the largest young population in the world—542 million people in India are less than 24 years old. Exploiting this demographic dividend requires significant investment in all levels of education. India's per capita public expenditure on education as a percentage of GDP is amongst the lowest in the world. While 96.5% of children from ages 6 to 14 are enrolled in school, many do not receive quality education. In 2010, only 20% of children in Grade 3 were able to read a text of Grade 2 difficulty. In fact, even by Grade 5, only 53% of children were able to read a Grade text. Even though the public expenditure per student enrolled in government schools is relatively high, education outcomes are uneven.

Policy Enablers and Barriers Formal schools are highly regulated; long-standing rules mandate all formal educational institutes to operate as not-for-profit institutions. In contrast, the private coaching and education content space is unregulated. The flow of equity capital to the formal education space is limited as not-for profit structures offer limited financial return to investors. Since formal schools require substantial access to capital this creates constraints for SEs. In order to attract equity capital, many affordable schools operate a two-tier structure, in which the school is a not-for-profit entity, but the school management company is a for-profit entity; equity investments take place in the for-profit entity.

Though many affordable schools have a two-tiered structure to access equity capital, many schools depend on debt capital for scale. In order to leverage the infrastructure of mainstream private schools to benefit the poor, the government has instituted the Right for Education Act that mandates private schools to provide 25% of their seats for low income households with expenses for these seats covered by the government. However, this policy is yet to be implemented as its facing stiff opposition from school managements, parents, and even some politicians who have stakes in schools.

Energy

Overview and Need Assessment

Uniform access to energy is an essential part of sustainable development. In India, the access to the energy landscape is skewed as a result of poor energy distribution in rural parts of the country. This is mainly due to the financial infeasibility of laying expensive electric cables to reach remote areas that only cover small populations. According to the National Sample Survey of 2007, approximately 75% of villages are electrified, but only 50–55% of households have access to electricity. Rural populations primarily rely on kerosene for lighting and biomass for cooking. The situation of unequal access to energy is compounded by the fact that there is around 9% shortage in current energy capacity.

India needs an additional 80,000 million units of power capacity to satisfy its energy demand and improved distribution systems to minimize transmission losses. It is estimated that rural consumers across India spend about $4.86 billion per year on energy.

Energy sources used by rural populations are not only inefficient but also cause significant environmental and health problems. The underpenetrated energy market offers immense potential for product interventions. SEs enter this space with the objective of enabling access to environmentally friendly, affordable energy.

SE Involvement in the Sector

SEs primarily focus on off-grid/distributable renewable energy and waste-to-energy projects. Energy-centric SEs require a substantial amount of capital for power generation, product development, and distribution, causing these SEs to be structured as for-profit entities. Enterprises also adopt innovative distribution models to reach the end consumer. SEs focused on underserved populations that are still in the early stages of development. Thus, the revenue, scale, and profitability of the enterprises are relatively small. The space has both niche players such as Husk Power and Desi Power, and large corporations like Tata BP Solar, Philips, and Schneider.

Policy Enablers and Barriers

The government is encouraging the participation of private suppliers across all sectors of energy through progressive policies and schemes. Some of key regulatory enablers in the energy sector are:

1. No approval required for setting up mini-grids delivering power within a 3km radius
2. Capital subsidies for mini-grid technologies and solar products
3. Budgetary allocation of $6.2 billion for rural electrification

A $688 million fund for clean energy. The regulations in the energy space act both as enablers and inhibitors of growth. For instance, though the government has removed the need to obtain approvals for mini-grids, getting a commencement approval is time consuming and requires communicating with several departments. Some of the other key regulations that negatively impact the sector are the high import duty on solar products, hardware compliance tests necessary to acquire subsidies, and subsides for competitive products such as kerosene.

Despite some regulatory inhibitors, the space has witnessed a significant flow of capital as private equity investments in clean energy grew from $851 million in 2005 to $2.1 billion in 2008 before witnessing a slowdown due to the financial crisis. However, the potential untapped opportunity for investors in clean energy sources for rural consumers is about $2.1 billion per annum.

Financial Inclusion

Overview and Need Assessment

Access to finance by the underserved is an essential prerequisite for inclusive growth. Currently, only 10% of the total demand for microcredit is met by MFIs.

Moreover, this gap is concentrated in India's northeastern Hindi-speaking belt. In the Indian state of Uttar Pradesh, only 1.5% of total microcredit demand has been met. The underserved also have limited access to other financial services such as micro-savings and micro-insurance products.

SE Involvement in the Financial Inclusion Sector

Microfinance Institutions (MFIs) act as financial intermediaries with products and processes geared towards serving vulnerable sections of the society. MFIs in India started out as not-for-profit entities that provided standardized credit products. As the credit portfolio of MFIs grew rapidly, access to capital became vital. Since not-for-profits cannot legally attract equity investments, most MFIs transitioned into a for-profit model, usually structuring themselves as Non-banking Financial Companies (NBFCs). The NBFC structure enabled access to both debt and equity funds. Currently, an estimated 300 institutions provide loans to low-income households for income generating activities, with a client base of 27 million active borrowers and $4.5 billion in outstanding loans. The Self-Help Group Bank Linkage Program promotes financial transactions between commercial banks and self-help groups (SHGs). In addition to the commercial banks, the other key stakeholder in the SHG Bank Linkage Program is a not-for-profit organization that promotes the members of the SHG. The bank linkage model works on the principle of community ownership; no profit-oriented delivery model exists in this space. Currently, there are about 7 million SHGs linked to banks through this program. Branchless banking is another relatively new strategy in the financial inclusion space. Enterprises in the branchless banking space use technology (smart cards or mobile phones) to facilitate access to finance for under-banked populations. Branchless banking SEs are structured as for-profit entities as the technology infrastructure and management require significant capital. The rapid growth of the financial inclusion space has attracted the attention of equity and debt investors. Over the last three years, many mainstream investors actively invested in large for-profit MFIs. SKS Microfinance was the first MFI to go public; it raised $367 million through a public issue. Bank lending to MFIs increased 2.8 times from $1.1 billion in March 2009 to $3.2 billion in March2010.

CHAPTER-III

Multidimensional Aspects of Cooperative Entrepreneurship Development Systems and Programs

The entrepreneurship development system through cooperative approach shall remain the main focus for cooperative business development in the new century. The seventh principle of cooperation "concern for community" shall also be the guiding principle in the designing and implementing the entrepreneurship system. Hitherto, many number of activities (service) done by cooperative movement cannot succeed unless they develop proper cooperative entrepreneurship system. Allied activities and industrial development and many other ventures would eventually depend on entrepreneurship development system. But no one exact idea (or) development dictum for innovative measures for cooperative entrepreneurs can be used; it must be multi-faceted and multi-dimensional in approach. At any cost, cooperative approach of entrepreneurship system can be even better utilized to deliver the essential goods and services than the public sector undertakings by retaining the multi-dimensional aspects of Cooperative Entrepreneurship Development.

Why do we Need Cooperative Entrepreneurship System?

It is essential to have enabling policy environment which can be evolved (or is being) created through the harmonization of cooperative regulatory system/frameworks at national, regional and global levels to promote the most effective and efficient cooperative entrepreneurship system. In order to satisfy the needs of an increasingly more sophisticated membership, agricultural farmers and highly competitive globalised market environment, cooperative right now must be imbibe and inculcate the culture of strategic management like any other business enterprises, and must provide its members and public at large verities of new products and services. In this era of economic reforms and globalised environment, it is essential and imperative for the cooperative organization to provide its members, stakeholders and customer with high quality of goods and services and make their organization more viable, productive and profitable.

What cooperative entrepreneurship seeks to achieve in the long run is to inject into the cooperative movement viable creativity and high level of innovative market orientation through effective and efficient strategic management approaches. For cooperative organizations to be highly entrepreneurial, they must imbibe and incorporate all of the following ingredients as the main posture of entrepreneurship approach viz. They must be creative, innovative and proactive and calculated (management) risk takers, they must adopt creative innovative approach, proactive and calculated risk takers, and they must add value to their products. Cooperative organizations must be driven by emerging open market opportunities, capturing market shares and customer (satisfaction) preferences. Adoption of business like (approach) in their decision making processes, they must reduce all cost of production, and they must achieve higher efficiency in the production of goods and services. Finally, all cooperative organizations must enhance, production of high quality of goods and service to enable them capture new customers and compete in the open market economy.

If cooperative organizations are driven by the urge of gaining profit and positive growth of business dealing, then their members can optimize their socio-economic welfare and benefits in the long-run. This can be balanced with the service motive of cooperative organizations.

Essential Elements of Entrepreneurial Development Programme through Cooperative Approach

Development of capture entrepreneur means inculcating entrepreneurial traits and skills to the active entrepreneur by imparting the required knowledge, development of the technical, financial, marketing and managerial skills and building the entrepreneurial attitude, among the cooperative entrepreneurs and members of cooperative organizations.

The process of entrepreneurial development involves equipping a person with the information used for enterprises building and sharpening his entrepreneurial skills. Entrepreneurial development programme may be defined as "a programme designed to help an individual in strengthening his entrepreneurial motive and in acquiring skills and capabilities necessary for playing his entrepreneurial role effectively. It is necessary to promote his understanding of motives and their impact on entrepreneurial values and behaviour for this purpose". The man objectives of an entrepreneurial development programme as follows:

- To identify and train potential cooperative entrepreneurs.
- To develop necessary knowledge and skills among the participants.
- To impart basic managerial understanding and strategies for overall management and administration.
- To provide post training assistance and provide technical support system.

In order to fulfill the above objective, the most effective and efficient cooperative approaches are essential.

CHAPTER-IV

Functional areas of Management which can be offered through Cooperative Entrepreneurship Development System-Cooperative Marketing Approaches

The marketing concept consists of two phases:

i. Determining the needs, wants and values of customers in a target market

ii. Adapting the cooperative approach and network to deliver the goods services more effectively and efficiently even more than the existing middle men.

In today's world, cooperative organizations provide a highly competitive environment and produce goods to be sold in a larger market both coming from agricultural and non-agricultural sector. Any marketing process, whether it is simple (or) complex, whether it is performed by cooperatives (or) other forms of enterprises, involves the various marketing management functions such as grading, standardization, handling, storing, financing and risk-bearing etc. whoever performs these functions must see that they are performed in the most effective and efficient manner.

The service objective of cooperative organization does not in any way undermine the need for management orientation to the marketing function activities rather it supplements all the business activities. Generally, the ultimate aim of marketing is to assume a managerial role to coordinate all interacting activities with the objective of planning, promoting and distributing all consumers wants, satisfying products and services to the present and potential customers in the long-run.

With regards to entrepreneurial strategy of marketing approach, it is essential for the cooperative organizations to enhance the inspiration of locally produced goods which must be sold in other countries i.e., SAARC countries. The entrepreneurs must be taught all the parameters of marketing and marketing management. Also the practices and philosophy of cooperative marketing organizations must be instilled in their minds.

In a globalised market environment, numerous marketing strategies and methods are evolving and all the functional and managerial areas of enterprises are frequently changing. Cooperative marketing organizations have since been marketing the agricultural goods/ commodities, but now times have changed and they must make suitable arrangements for undertaking industrial marketing and deal with consumer goods, specific raw material etc. Thus, this kind of distribution and marketing by cooperative organizations can motivate the entrepreneurs and enthusiastically make them to start the business at gross-root level with less investment and higher productivity. Moreover, the economic liberalization policy has promoted the movement and marketing of all aspects of goods and services in any form of enterprise to another without many hurdles. Moreover the inter-enterprise transactions and transfer has been made free and possible. In this connection, cooperative marketing societies/ organizations should take adequate interest and obtain proper initiatives in carrying out all modes of Intra and Inter-enterprises business and also promote the culture of entrepreneurship development system among their federations, the cooperative union, cooperative societies (primaries) and members.

The financial assistance through NCDC for various Processing and Industrial Cooperatives in order to attained viable in economic and social for every members. If the share value is remaining high from Govt, we cannot achieved anything from cooperative sector include Entrepreneurship.

Human Resource Management Strategies for Cooperative Entrepreneurship

The application of HRD strategies in cooperatives organizations means that the manpower input to cooperative sector must be planned and the information on manpower gathered and organized, coordinated, controlled, communicated, carryout all manpower budgeted information, and management system. Education and training of cooperative employees, mobilization of qualified and skilled workers, and manpower development activities must be effectively and efficiently undertaken by cooperative organization capable of providing goods and services required by their members and customers at large.

The fast downing of next millennium and ever dynamic socio-economic changes taking place in the dynamic economic environment have deeply pressurized policy makers/ politicians/Government authorities to redefine the concept of human resource development in order to cater to relevant needs and aspiration of cooperators and their cooperatives organizations. There is very high expectation on cooperatives as a result of the present economic environment which require cooperatives in the future to assume greater and wider responsibilities in amelioration of the socio-economic conditions of members. There is an urgent need for intensified training and educational programmes to meet the emerging needs of cooperative sector and mobilization of manpower development programmes. Cooperative members and employees and particularly women and youth must be given greater extent to participation and awareness of the practices and philosophy of cooperatives to involve them more actively in the cooperative business affairs in the long-run. For so many years, women and youth have been over looked, but they play greater role in promoting cooperative movement and are also essential for the overall success and development of cooperative movement in the new centenary. Therefore, they must be included fully in the Cooperative Entrepreneurship Development System.

Thus, HRD programmes/scheme in cooperative entrepreneurship system is the corner stone of the cooperative entrepreneurship development process. Because, the maneuver of systematic knowledge of entrepreneurial skill is gained by the direct improvement of the human resource/manpower of cooperative organizations. Now-a-days, the "Brain-Drain" and "contract system" is directly (or) indirectly causing concern in most of the organizations, especially on the technological background of the manpower. Thus, cooperative organizations should take the initiative for utilization of human resource from other organizations (outsourcing) and ensure maximum, efficient and effective manpower input to serve the cooperative organizations.

Reforming Cooperative Credit Structure in India for Financial Inclusion

Present Status of Cooperatives

The growth and advancement of Indian cooperative systems have been rapid over the years, and cooperatives have substantially increased their presence by adding more branches and members as well as expanding business in both credit and non-credit activities. According to the National Federation of State Cooperative Banks (NAFSCOB), as of March 31, 2012, the total number of state cooperative banks (STCBs) in the country was 31 and the total number of their branches 1047. The total number of district cooperative banks in India was 371, and the total number of branches 13495.

The financial performance of the cooperative banks can be captured by two critical indicators, deposits and credit. An examination of available data reveals that total deposit had fallen by 3.7 percent in 2010-11 compared to 2009-10 figures but there was a growth of 6 percent in the following year, i.e., between 2010-11 to 2011-12. Though uneven across years, growth figures witnessed in recent years have been positive. The total loans issued by cooperative banks increased by 19 percent in 2011-12 compared to the previous year. However, there was a perceptible decrease in the demand for loans from lower-tier institutions. Despite this, short and long term loans together disbursed for 2011-12 registered an increase of 16 percent, compared to the previous year. The banks have also gone for investment related activities in the form of statutory (SLR) investments, which constitute more than 60 percent of the total investment of the STCCS. The total borrowings of the SCBs in 2011–12 also witnessed an increase of 31 percent.

The financial position of most of the District Central Cooperative Banks (DCCBs) is similar to that of State Cooperative Banks, with positive growth in deposits and credit, and most of them have been earning profits. The third and the lowest tier in the short term credit system at the rural level is the Primary Agriculture Credit Societies (PACS). The examination of data of PACS at a national level reveals that the total membership for 2011- 2012 was 127.4 million (NAFSCOB, 2012) and the number of total borrowers was 45.2 million individuals, and total deposit 189760 million rupees for 2012. Corresponding figures for some of the previous years, for example, for 2004-2005 are: total membership of PACS 135.4 million individuals; number of borrowing members 51.3 million, and total deposit 181430 million rupees. Although the total numbers of borrowers had fallen, interestingly the total deposit had increased in the same period.

The data revealed that southern states had the highest number of members per PACS at 3256 (NAFSCOB 2012). The western states had the lowest number of members at 577 persons per PACS. Further, the low number of members per PACS in the western states could be because of the relatively higher number of PACS located in these states. The average number of borrowers per PACS is 507 across India, with the highest number of borrowers being in the southern region with 1514 persons and the lowest number of borrowers from the north-eastern region with 61 persons (See table 1.1).

Distributions of PACS by Region, 2011-12

Regions	Total Number of PACS	Average Membership per PACS	Average Borrowing Membership Per PACS	Credit Potential Available
Northern	10818	922	567	355
Eastern	19421	1417	401	1016
Central	15357	697	331	366
Western	29633	577	166	411
Southern	13703	3256	1514	1742
North Eastern	3500	1133	61	1072

Source: NAFSCOB 2011 – 2012

The gap between the average membership and average borrowing membership is indicative of the borrowing capacity available (demand for loan) and the availability of potential credit. In essence, there is a huge potential for expansion of credit, more so in the southern, eastern and north-eastern regions. The southern region holds the highest potential of credit at 1742 individual members in each society. Similarly the potential for credit stands at 1072 individual members in the north-eastern and at 1016 individual members in the eastern region for each cooperative society.

The cooperative credit institutions have undergone a substantial transformation over the years in terms of organisational structure in the rural and urban areas. However, there are certain critical problems in their functioning still persisting which make them (especially at the rural level) *non viable institutions*. A large number of PACS becoming loss-making entities across the country is a testimony of this fact. The Vaidyanathan Committee was appointed to outline a revival package for cooperatives as the finances of most cooperatives had deteriorated.

Functions and Operation of STCCS

The mandate and operational details of STCCS vary across states depending on the structure governing these institutions in the concerned state. However, the main purpose of STCCS is to provide credit and monitor the lower tiers of the cooperative institutions. Even if, these institutions are controlled by multiple agencies and they still have the freedom to expand their activities. After the entry of commercial banks and RRBs, the role of cooperative institutions as major suppliers of short-term credit has declined and in their place, commercial banks and RRBs have become the major suppliers of short-term credit. In the current competitive environment, STCCS have necessarily to compete with the other financial institutions, particularly regional rural banks (RRBs).

Notwithstanding the increased competition, the cooperative banking sector has been registering positive growth; for instance the number of functioning offices of short term cooperative banks (STCB) branches have increased in the last ten years, i.e., from 986 in 1998-99 to 1015 by 2009 -10, though the growth rate varied across states for several reasons. Further, the average annual percentage growth rates of offices and membership for the period 1999-00 to 2011-12 were 1.7 and 6.47 percent, respectively (see Table 2.1). Also, the annual average growth in membership per office has increased; in fact, the average annual percent increment in members per office has been 4.73 (from 199-00 to 2011-12). Similarly, there was an increase in the total paid share capital of the state cooperative banks (SCBs), which in turn brought down the share of the state government contribution to 11 percent.

Annual Growth Rates of Offices and Membership of SCBs

Year	Annual Growth Rate of		
	No. of Offices	Total Membership	Members per Office
1999-00	2.85	-5.27	-7.6
2000-01	-0.23	-10.52	-10.13
2001-02	3.93	-4.02	-7.75
2002 - 03	3.56	13.74	9.92
2003 - 04	-0.21	12.93	13.19
2004 - 05	2.58	3.74	1.13
2005 - 06	0.94	-1.87	-2.79
2006 - 07	-2.49	-3.21	-0.73
2007 - 08	5.12	1.44	-3.50
2008 - 09	0.61	33.03	32.23
2009 - 10	2.32	64.77	61.03
2010 - 11	1.28	-29.01	-29.91
2011 - 12	1.85	8.32	6.35
AAGR	**1.70**	**6.47**	**4.73**

Note: AAGR: Annual Average Growth Rate in terms of percent increment

Source: Computed using data from various National Federation of State Cooperative Banks (NAFSCOB) Reports.

In regard to financial indicators, deposits in state cooperative banks (SCBs) in the country aggregated at Rs.84837 crore[2] during 2009-10, representing an increase of 18.2 percent over the previous year (see National Federation of State Cooperative Banks (NAFSCOB), 2009-10), though the increased deposits did not lead to increased lending. For instance, during 2003-04, there was negative growth in aggregate loans issued, while this trend was reversed during 2006-07 to 2007-08, the growth rate being 13.26 percent for the period. At a disaggregated level, out of 31 short-term cooperative banks (STCBs), 14 recorded negative growth, while the others recorded a positive growth rate during the period. Also, the ratio of the non performing assets (NPAs) to loan outstanding varied from 17 to 11 percent, which is attributed to various factors including the government's interest subsidized credit programme (NAFSCOB,2009-10). However, it is somewhat encouraging to observe that the NPAs to total loan outstanding ratio, which was around 17.2 percent during 2002-03, declined to 11.6 per cent by 2009-10 (Table

2.2). This may be to some extent due to the application of Agriculture Debt Weaver & Debt Relief Scheme.

NPAs and Loan Outstanding of SCBs (Rs. Crore)

Year	Total NPAs	Total Loan Outstanding	NPAs to Loan Outstanding Ratio (Percent)
2000-01	3889	29848	13.03
2001-02	4485	32111	13.97
2002-03	6284	32798	19.16
2003-04	6548	35105	18.65
2004-05	6072	37346	16.26
2005-06	6735	39684	16.97
2006-07	6704	47354	14.16
2007-08	6169	48228	12.79
2008-09	5718	46201	12.38
2009-10	5432	49104	11.06

Note: Rs 1 Crore = Rs 10,000,000.

Source: NAFSCOB Report: Various issues

District Central Cooperative Banks (DCCBs)

The district central cooperative banks, as the name suggests, are operational at the district level under the guidance of SCB. At the national level, the total numbers of DCCBs as well as their branches increased marginally during the period 1998-99 – 2007- 08, while the membership per branch increased considerably from 6233 to 9140. Similarly, the aggregate paid-up share capital also recorded an increase of 6 percent. The contribution of state government towards share capital has come down marginally over the years, and currently accounts for 11 percent. The aggregate deposits of DCCBs stood at Rs. 105594 crores during 2007-08, of which 62 percent of deposits was held by five states: Maharashtra, Kerala, Tamil Nadu, Gujarat and Uttar Pradesh in descending order, thereby showing concentration of cooperative activities in selected states. The aggregate outstanding loan also showed an increasing trend, the annual average percentage increment of loan outstanding during the 2001-2008 period being 9.98 (NAFCOSB 2007-2008).

Ironically, however, the NPA ratios for DCCBs had shown generally an increasing trend between 2000- 01 and 2007-08 (Table 2.3). The rate of growth of NPAs was relatively higher than the growth in total advances during this period. The growth in 'loss' assets have also been comparatively higher than the other two asset categories for DCCBs which is a matter of serious concern.

Annual Growth Rate of Asset-Quality of DCCBs

Annual Growth Rate of

Year	Sub Standard Assets	Doubtful Assets	Loss Assets	Total NPA
2001-02	26.65	22.48	39.19	26.33
2002-03	20.21	19.20	-5.44	17.10
2003-04	10.85	19.92	37.45	16.46
2004-05	-23.26	-0.25	21.30	-10.06
2005-06	6.76	10.67	5.35	8.19
2006-07	-7.68	14.17	17.33	5.00
2007-08	23.26	7.35	7.65	13.54
AAGR	**8.11**	**13.36**	**17.55**	**10.94**

Note: AAGR-Average Annual Growth Rate, Growth Rates measured in terms of percent increment

Source: Computed using data from NAFSCOB

Primary Agricultural Credit Societies (PACS)

Primary Agricultural Credit Societies (PACS) form the third and bottom tier of the short-term credit cooperative structure and operates at the grassroots level, i.e., at the village level. As PACs are the direct purveyors of credit to the rural borrowers, both coverage and viability of these institutions need to be strengthened in order to ensure inclusive financial assistance to the needy, as well as to enhance the stability of the short-term cooperative credit structure. As revealed by the study, over the last twelve years, on an average the number of PACS has been declining, but the membership has been marginally increasing (see the last row depicting average annual growth). According to NAFSCOB, membership increased from 12.5 crores during 2005 -06 to 13.3 crores during 2008-9, only to decline to 12.6 crores during 2009-10.

Annual Growth Rate (percent increment) of Membership of PACS

Year	Annual Growth Rate		
	No. of Societies	Total Membership	Members per Society
2000 - 01	-2.66	-8.00	-5.35
2001 - 02	-0.6	2.22	2.84
2002 - 03	14.31	20.96	5.82
2003 - 04	-5.85	9.60	16.41
2004 - 05	3.82	-5.91	-9.38
2005 - 06	-3.09	-1.73	1.40
2006 - 07	-12.37	0.48	14.66
2007 - 08	1.85	4.42	2.52
2008 - 09	0.72	0.76	0.04
2009 - 10	-1.03	-4.48	-3.49
2010 - 11	-1.30	-4.11	-2.84
2011 - 12	-1.05	-6.29	-5.30
AAGR	**-0.60**	**0.66**	**1.44**

Note: AAGR: Annual Average Growth Rate

Source: NAFSCOB

More importantly, the number of borrowers as a percentage of the total members increased from 37 to 60.4 during the above period. Moving on to the financial indicators, one observes that deposits as well as borrowings increased by 5 and 17 percent respectively during the above period, and as expected, a positive link is discernible between deposits and loans issued (see Table 2.5).

An important observation from our analysis of NAFSCOB data is that the quantum of over-dues as a percentage of total outstanding loans, which is a rough indicator of the non-performing assets of PACS, was high across all three tiers of the short- term cooperative credit structure.

Moreover, there was a sharp increase in this ratio from 26.9 percent in March 2007 to 36.6 percent in March 2008.

As observed from the above analysis, possibly owing to consolidation and restructuring, there has been a reduction in the number of institutions at the 3rd tier level. This has resulted in the share of loans and deposits at the PACS level increasing in recent years, as evidenced by the rise in the total membership as well as borrowers in PACS, which is the lowest tier in the rural cooperative credit structure. Ironically, however, high levels of NPAs continue to affect the rural cooperative sector. This disturbing issue needs to be tackled effectively in order to make cooperative banking institutions successful in the days to come.

Task Force Recommendations on Revival of STCCS

In view of the importance of the cooperative credit structure in India and the gloomy state in which it is currently, the Government of India (GOI) has been making concerted efforts to revitalize the system. As an essential step, GOI appointed a Task Force in August 2004 under the chairmanship of Prof. A.Vaidyanathan with the mandate to formulate a plan of action to rejuvenate the rural cooperative credit structure. The Task Force realized that a solely market driven institution cannot take care of the needs of the poor and the needy in a federal structure like India, and recommended that the state governments also need to be incorporated into this process. With this objective, members of the Task Force held lengthy consultations with governments at both the centre and states in order to work out modalities for the implementation of the plan. The committee's final report on STCCS was submitted in February 2005.

The new economic policies have been successful in unshackling private enterprises from the earlier rigid dispensation and promoting industrial and services sectors to ensure higher economic growth in these sectors. Sadly, the agricultural sector did not get much attention compared to the other two sectors, and therefore the positive benefits of the economic growth remained out of reach of the needy masses in rural India. However, in the first two decades of the new economic policy, in spite of its predominant role in delivering credit and non credit facilities to the lower segment of the economy, the cooperative sector did not receive enough attention. The paradigm shift in Indian discourse created scores of new challenges for the cooperative sector. Prior to the onset of economic reforms, cooperative credit institutions were financially weak and also operationally inefficient. Several times in the past, committees were formed to reform these institutions, and based on their recommendations various steps were taken at different points in time to improve operations.

The Need for Task Force Committee

Since independence, the state policy was mainly focused on creating rapid and equitable economic development. As a part of this strategy, governments at both the centre and states embarked on a number of policies for reforming and streamlining rural financial cooperatives, and several committees were formed to arrive at appropriate policies for improving the sector. The All India Rural Credit Survey (AIRCS) recommended state partnership in terms of both equity and governance and management. It also recommended to make a link between credit and marketing cooperatives and to enlarge their areas of operation. Importantly in its recommendations, the AIRCS strongly opposed direct government intervention in the governance and management of cooperative credit institutions. As a result, the view that government should restrict itself to ensuring that there is continuous flow of cheap institutional credit to the cooperative institutions and that government should not intervene in their operations unless these institutions failed to deliver institutional credits in the rural areas became forceful. Down the road, the Bawa Committee (1971) recommended setting up large multi-purpose cooperatives in tribal areas. In 1975, the Hazari Committee recommended integration of short term and long term credit structures. The National Commission on Agricultural which was formed one year later recommended setting up Farmers Service Cooperative Societies with the active collaboration of nationalized banks. Later, in 1981, the Committee to Review Arrangements for Institutional Credit for Agriculture and Rural Development (CRAFICARD, which is also known as Sivaraman Committee), recommended setting up NABARD.

The state's heightened interest in and concern for the performance of cooperatives in the country became obvious. The focus, however, was on expanding and reorganizing the state supported structures, without first addressing the task of restoring and strengthening autonomy, mutual help and self-governance. The Agriculture Credit Review Committee (Khusro Committee, 1989) talked for the first time about the importance of encouraging member thrift and savings for the cooperatives. Of these, special mention needs to be made of the Committees headed by Chaudhry Brahm Perkash, Shri Jagdish Capoor, Sri Vikhe Patil, Prof. V.S. Vyas and Prof. A. Vaidyanathan during the last two decades, to suggest reforms in the cooperative credit sector. The Sri Brahm Perkash committee emphasized the need to make the cooperatives self-reliant, autonomous and fully democratic institutions and proposed a model law. The Jagadish Capoor committee recommended measures for improvement of human resources in the cooperative structure.

Policy Recommendations of the Task Force

Some of the important recommendations of the Task Force include:

- All users including depositors should have full voting rights
- Cooperative institutions should have autonomy to deal with administrative and financial matters
- Government should not nominate any representative(s) on the Boards of cooperatives, and provision for government equity should be removed
- Restrictive orders on financial issues need to be withdrawn
- Cooperatives should have freedom for both taking loans from and placing deposits with any financial institution of their choice Permitting cooperatives under the parallel Acts to be members of upper tiers under the existing cooperative societies Acts
- A cap on the powers of state governments is needed to reduce the government interference on Boards
- Elections should be conducted in a timely manner, and prior to the expiry of the existing Boards
- To ensure smooth progress of the cooperative banks, RBI should have full regulatory powers
- To prescribe prudential norms including CRAR for all financial cooperatives including PACS.

Policy Package

To execute the recommendations of the Task Force, the Government of India (GOI) created National Bank for Agriculture and Rural Development (NABARD) as the implementing agency, and also announced a financial assistance package. Besides these two steps, GOI also prescribed several other mandatory requirements such as legal and institutional reforms and improvement of management of the cooperative institutions.

Financial Assistance

The financial assistance package was to encourage state governments to reform their legal and institutional system by incorporating the recommendations of the Task Force. By using this assistance package, it became possible to cover accumulated losses in the Cooperative Credit Societies (CCS), but the institutions were barred from writing off the existing loans, and the cooperatives were advised to make efforts to recover outstanding loans in order to make the institutions financially sound. The first step of the financial restructuring process was to ensure the financial health of the Primary Agricultural Cooperative Societies (PACS) . The method suggested was to cleanse the balance sheets and strengthen the capital base of PACS, so that they could move on to the upper tiers. With this, the DCCBs would become eligible to receive assistance in order to clear the existing accumulated losses and reach a minimum norm of capital adequacy. The same process was also prescribed to recover the financial health of the State Cooperative Banks (SCBs). Accumulated losses in the CCS include the items listed below:

- Non-repayment of loans disbursed by cooperatives for agricultural and other businesses purposes;
- Non-repayment of loans to individuals for other purposes like consumer goods, housing, gold loans etc.
- Losses on account of non-credit businesses like public distribution system (PDS), procurement of food grains on behalf of government, sale of fertilizers etc.
- Non-repayment of loans issued under government guarantees where the State government has not yet paid to the cooperatives although guarantees have been invoked/ un-invoked;
- Non-payment of dues by governments on account of waivers or subsidies announced by them; and Losses due to fraud etc.

Legal and Institutional Reforms

The revival package for STCCS focuses on introducing legal and institutional reforms which will enable the cooperatives to function as autonomous member-centric and member-governed institutions. Suitable amendments of Acts, such as Cooperative Societies Acts of the States, Banking Regulations (BR) Act, NABARD Act, and DICGC Act are to be made.

Reforms in the Cooperative Societies Act: To make the process faster, the state governments should issue Executive Orders to bring in the structural reforms in credit cooperatives by stipulating the following provisions:

- Full voting rights need to be ensured to all users of financial services including depositors in cooperatives other than cooperative banks.
- There should not be any form of state interference in financial and administrative issues of the cooperatives.
- The state government should put a cap of 25 percent on equity. It should also have the right to lower it further. Besides this, the state governments should not nominate more than one representative on the Boards of cooperative banks.

- Wherever applicable, cooperatives registered under the State Cooperative Societies Act should not face any difficulty to migrate to the Parallel Act.

- All restrictive orders related to financial issues need to be withdrawn.

- All cooperatives should have freedom to take loans from any regulated financial institution of their choice and should be able to deposit funds in such financial institutions of their choice. Here, state governments/RCS can determine a threshold limit for such activities. There should not be any restriction on cooperatives under the Parallel Act to become members of upper tiers under the existing Cooperative Societies Acts and vice versa.

- State governments should not be able to easily surpass the Boards.

- Elections should be held in a timely manner, and necessarily before the expiry of the existing Boards.

- To ensure smooth progress of the cooperative banks, RBI should have full regulatory powers

- Prudential norms should be prescribed including CRAR, for all financial cooperatives including PACS, as per the directions of RBI.

The Task Force recommended a model Cooperative Law for adoption by the state governments. And, in such states where an old Cooperative Societies Act is in force, convergence of the existing and the recommended Acts should be attempted in order to make the Act purposeful and compliant to relevant laws. However, if any state is unwilling to adopt the model act in total, then it should incorporate the salient provisions of the model act into the existing Cooperative Societies Acts.

Reforms in the Banking Regulation (BR) Act of 1949: Amendments made to the BR Act included the following:

- All cooperative banks and commercial banks should have the same regulatory norms.

- Regardless of the type of membership of cooperatives including membership of the DCCBs and SCBs, RBI should prescribe criteria for election to Boards of cooperative banks.

- The RBI should prescribe criteria for professionals to be on the Boards of cooperative banks. In case members with such professional qualifications or experience do not get elected in the normal electoral process, then the Board will be required to co-opt such professionals to the Board and they would have full voting rights.

- The cooperative banks themselves should appoint their CEOs without having any interference by the State government. However, RBI may prescribe the minimum qualifications of the CEO to be appointed and the name proposed by the cooperative bank for the position of CEO would have to be approved by RBI.

- Cooperatives other than cooperative banks, as approved by the RBI, shall not accept deposits of non-voting members. Such cooperatives should also not use words like "bank", "banking", "banker" or any other derivative of the word "bank" in their registered name.

- Introducing a Common Accounting System (CAS). At the primary level, the CAS also needs to be simple and easily comprehensible, and facilitate a sound Management Information System (MIS) across various levels of STCCS and beyond, to facilitate proper and timely decisions at all levels. The CAS and MIS so evolved would form the basis for computerization of STCCS units.

Improvement in Management Quality

Capacity building and training: Quite often, the Board of Directors, vested with the responsibility of business development and management, are also not sufficiently conversant with issues relating to banking business, and corporate governance. Also, in most institutions there is neither any systematic arrangement to impart basic competency to the staff at entry level nor any familiarization or sensitization programme for the Board members. Hence, training was recommended at all the levels of personnel including the Board members.

Computerization of PACS: The present competitive business environment and changing market dynamics, fresh regulations and compliance requirements, industry consolidation, need for delivery of cost effective products and services, maintaining secure data platforms, meeting increasing customer demands and other strategic issues have all made banking far more complex than in the past. As such the use of technology has become a key focus area for extending the outreach of banking and financial services.

Considering the fact that the STCCS could not realize the enormous potential opened up by its vast outreach owing mainly to a "deep impairment of governance", a task force was constituted in order to improve the functioning of the institution. The task force made a series of recommendations to enhance the autonomy of the institution especially at the village level, and to ensure better governance. A financial package has also been devised depending on the level of non-performing assets of the banks. The above statements are mandated to critically examine the process of implementation of the recommendations of the task force in the state of Bihar and suggest areas that need further strengthening in order to make this revival effort a success.

Financial Strategy for Developing Cooperative Entrepreneurship

Finance is the lubricant and motive power that rotates the wheels of all cooperative business organizations. Financial management of cooperative organizations has a profound impact on the business efficiency, productivity of cooperative and profitability of cooperative enterprises. Generally, the "cooperative finance" denotes the provision of funds for certain specific purposes at a time when it is needed and at the required amount (magnitude). Moreover, business finance is "that business activity which is concerned with the acquisition and conservation of capital funds in meeting financial needs and overall objectives of the firm". In order to meet the funds for cooperative entrepreneurship development system, the following are the major sources:

Cooperative organizations can allocate specific amount of money for cooperative entrepreneurship development by creating cooperative entrepreneurship development funds (CEDF). Subsequently, funds can be generated from private sector, public sector, multinational corporations, United Nation Industrial Development Organizations (UNIDO), International Banking Organizations, Non-Government organizations etc., to generate and contribute funds to be utilized for the overall entrepreneurship development activities and even the income tax exemption would be sought for contribution to these type of funds etc., Also NABARD and other financial agencies can assist in creating and contributing to cooperative entrepreneurship development funds. Soft (easy) terms and conditions of loan can be offered to cooperative entrepreneurs i.e., loans can be given at the lowest rate of interest.

Liberalized Financial Environment as Source of Financial Intermediation (Foreign Direct Investment) for Developing Cooperative Entrepreneurships

As investment portfolios have become increasingly global, most investors as well as governments are now seeking to attract foreign direct investment. All the investors must have a good working knowledge and understanding about the trends in the foreign aspects of investment and also the investment portfolios which involve risks in undertaking such investments in the future.

The keen interest of the government in FDI is also part of a broader interest in the forces propelling the ongoing integration of the world economy, or what is popularly described as "globalization". The scope and importance of foreign direct investment owned production and distribution facilities in most countries are cited as tangible evidence of globalization. Foreign direct investment is also viewed as a way of increasing the efficiency with which the world's scarce resources are used. A recent and specific example is the perceived role of FDI in efforts to stimulate economic growth in many of the world's poorest countries.

The investment funds can be obtained from FDI and they can start-up new colleges and universities for offering Specialized and Expertise knowledge in Cooperative Management, Training and Education of cooperative manpower. They can impart both the skills and knowledge of the latest technology and development. They can charge reasonable fees/payment for training and education of cooperative employees on the latest modem management and administration of business enterprises.

FDI can be encouraged through cooperative sector for transferring technology to the host countries, expanding trade, creating jobs and integration into global markets. By involving the cooperative sector, the country can adopt development strategies based on increased integration in the global market, and reap the benefits of globalization through investment in cooperative sector.

But, majority of the remaining cooperative organizations are expecting money from other agencies (or) Government, when we compare to other developed and even other developing countries which have a lot of surplus funds available at their disposal. Like, Canada, Japan, Denmark, Sweden etc., all those countries provide funds at low rate of interest and therefore, they can even be asked to circulate (or) invest these funds in Indian cooperative institutions at reasonable rate if interest and high rate of investment returns to the investors. Through this investment we shall have to strategically enlarge and provide enjoinment of cooperative entrepreneurial development programmes/system in the long run. Moreover, comprehensive, efficient and effective cooperative entrepreneurship system would involve and incorporate all activities suitable for globalised environment and liberalized policy of the economy.

Operational Strategy (OS) of Cooperative Entrepreneurship System

A strategy means "It is used to describe the direction that the organization chooses to follow in order to fulfill its mission" Bennet, R. In this sense it denotes that, cooperative entrepreneurship system must chalk-out an ideal direction and system to achieve the desired aims and mission of the organization in the long-run.

Every strategic plan must strive to strike a balance between many conflicting objectives, criteria and values and must consider the overall view from different strategical point of view. The cooperative organizations must have to evolve dynamic and comprehensive strategical approach in order to deliberately strive towards professionalization of management of CEDS. It is highly applicable for the development of cooperative entrepreneurship. The most effective and efficient operational strategies, are the most essential approaches in the twenty first century.

The operational strategies are understood through approaches such as cooperative marketing approach, Cooperative Business Finance approach, HRD approach, Management and administration approach, social ethical and moral approach, New Government policies and regulatory framework approach, linking cooperatives with global networks and encouraging the foreign direct investment (FDI) in the cooperative sector.

Operational Strategies (OS) in the Management and Administration of Cooperative Entrepreneurship

Operational strategies of cooperative entrepreneurship would include all the vital areas of administration and management of cooperative organizations. It would also include developing functional areas such as Finance, Marketing, Human Resource, Production Connection and information, legal, public relations, Education, Training, and leadership process.

All these strategies based on functional areas of management should raise the cooperatives multi-dimensional and multi-functional approaches in dealing with cooperative entrepreneurship. It covers various aspects of resource mobilization, sector wise advances, recovery of loans, and marketing, processing, budgeting and performance analysis of key result areas in the case of cooperative banking organizations. Moreover, the determination of SWOT analysis of cooperative entrepreneurship system would be delivered through formulating and tailoring the operational strategies (os) in the administration and management of the cooperative entrepreneurship systems are incorporated in the subsequent chapters.

Operational Strategies (OS) for Enhancing Social Ethics and Morals in Cooperative Entrepreneurship System

In the twenty first century, cooperative entrepreneurship must inculcate the spirit of social ethics, social morals, social norms, moral norms, ethical values, educational values etc. These are the major pillars in developing new generation cooperative entrepreneurship. All these factors are forming the major building blocks of successful cooperative enterprises. Cooperative enterprises are also imbibing the intricate values such as solidarity, equity, equality, fraternity, and social responsibility as stipulated and enunciated by the ICA cooperative principles and as practiced by cooperative organizations.

In the current scenario, many societies and communities in the world are encountering very huge barriers in trying to speed up socio-economic development. These barriers can be overcome by adopting suitable social ethics and imbibing deep source of human values in trying to achieve sustainable and viable means of exploitation of natural resources. The ultimate mission of cooperative movement is to enhance (or) raise the human values and integrity of human kind. At the same time, cooperative organizations can undertake numerous economic activities and commercial undertakings which are not causing deterioration of human values, reduction of environmental degradation and reduction of regional imbalances, adoption of pollution control measures etc.

Even the most important principle of cooperation has plainly elaborated the significance of **"concern for community"**. In other words, social ethical dimension and human prosperity can only be achieved in a collective manner with active community approach and complete participation in the long-run.

CHAPTER-V

Need for New Government Policies and Regulations in Favour of Cooperative Entrepreneurship System

Cooperative entrepreneurship system can be promoted by enacting favorable and conducive legal framework, favorable policy options and alternatives which are coopted and mainly entitled to strengthening of cooperative entrepreneurship. Even in the five year plans, coop entrepreneurship system or approaches in doing business must be given top priority and offered modem training techniques and methods. The government policies and measures in cooperative business affairs must be positive and must provide direction and inclination towards achieving higher viability, higher productivity and higher profitability in cooperative enterprises in the new millennium.

New approach and support model in formulating government policies towards cooperative entrepreneurship is highly essential and imperative in the new millennium. It can take the shape of up gradation, modernization, privatization of cooperative entrepreneurship system. But the privatization of cooperative entrepreneurship companies (or) units shall remain to be 49 percent of private share and all the remaining 51% share holding must be owned by the cooperative sector and Government through their own contributions. The Government must take steps again harmful bureaucratic style towards cooperative (or) set up of new cooperative organizational wing (CEDS) within the government system to look into the cooperative entrepreneurship business and it's affairs in the light of new economic environment and LPG's. But paradoxically, the government has encroached into active participation through high levels two-third of share value in every cooperative organization, as suggested and recommended by Dantwala Committee. This approach (Share Capital Participation and Control) might require immediate revising and re-vamping of the said recommendation, in the light of on-going new economic reforms.

The Government must permit and should allow profitable investment from direct foreign investment into cooperative sector to a certain percentage, especially those cooperative organizations dealing with industrial, services and high value agricultural commodities. Each and every member of cooperative, whatever (industrial (or) agricultural (or) processing etc.) must get concern on those areas which involve proper utilization of natural resources and accomplishment of all business connection and all entrepreneurial activities. The contribution of cooperative organization in the rural infrastructural development is very long obviously and the cooperative movement can give the first and top priority in the development of rural areas.

Those, rural population especially rural women, rural youth must initiate and undertake formation of cooperative entrepreneurial activities. In fact, cooperatives can develop proper communication, rural transportation etc., for the benefits of the rural communities.

For the success and growth of cooperative entrepreneurship system, these must be, at least good/cordial long term relationship between Government organizations and cooperative federations and their unions including primaries. It will enhance the long-term relationship and business activities within and outside these institutions in promoting entrepreneurs through Departments like Department of Industries and Commerce, Department of Agriculture and Animal Husbandry, Department of Marketing etc.

Policy Recommendation and Implication of Cooperative Entrepreneurship Development System

It is essential and imperative for the Cooperative Sector and also the Government to develop viable, productive and profitable cooperative entrepreneurship system to enable cooperative organizations to face new millennium with courage and determination.

The outcome of this research paper has provided an avenue for better policy options and alternatives to achieve this goal. They are as follows:

- There must be an effective and efficient training and education system to enhance cooperative entrepreneurship development system. Efforts must be taken by various organizations to promote Cooperative Entrepreneurship Development System (CEDS). Substantial number of organizations such as:
  - National Institute of Entrepreneurship and Small Business Development (NIESBUD).
  - Entrepreneurship Development Institute of India (EDII).
  - International Cooperative Alliance (ICA-ROAP).
  - Non-Governmental organizations and Developmental associations.
  - National Bank for Agriculture and Rural Development (NABARD).
  - Nehru Yuva Kendras (NYKS).
  - National Youth Cooperative Society (NYCS).
  - Committee for National Youth Programmes.
  - National Service Volunteer Scheme (NSVS).

- Have taken considerable efforts in imparting knowledge on entrepreneurship. Cooperative institutions, such as ICM (Pune), ICM, training institutes and regional training centers can offer effective and efficient training to the entrepreneurs.

- Strengthening and promoting innovation and creativity on the side of cooperative entrepreneurs are the sin-qua-non and fulcrum of cooperative entrepreneurship development system. In this way, they can undertake viable and profitable research and development activities in areas such as agro-industries, small-medium scale enterprises, micro enterprises, agro-based and food industry, Forest based industry, Mineral based industry, polymer and chemical based industries, Engineering and non-conventional energy, textile industry and service industries.

- E-Governance of cooperative organizations shall be the focus of the new millennium cooperatives organizations. The cooperative entrepreneurship development system would require imparting knowledge to the entrepreneurs on modernization, mechanization, and computerization of all business activities.

- In order to design, implement and develop cooperative entrepreneurship development system, there must be collaborative and cooperative attitude of all cooperative organizations such as, Federation (Apex), Unions, primaries.

- The Government wing dealing with cooperative affairs must provide leading role in promoting cooperative entrepreneurship system in coordination with cooperative movement itself to avoid duplication of functions and activities.

- It is essential to create harmonization of legal framework and regulations to provide linkages at the regional, state, national and global perspective. The policy enabling environment such as "New Policies and Government favorable attitude towards Cooperatives" can create better "modus-operandi" of cooperative entrepreneurship system.

- It is essential for cooperative organizations to do business like, activities and undertaking rational decisions which are promoting efficiency in production of goods and services, to reduce cost of production, enhance quality of products and services and meet the customers' preference and satisfaction in the long-run.

- It is essential to involve youth and women in cooperative entrepreneurship system. The present youth are well educated, computer literate, well informed in global affairs. Therefore, they must be made the main focus of the cooperative entrepreneurship development system.

- It is essential to create and develop strong, viable, productive and profitable finance and non-financial cooperative organization to facilitate strong frame work of CEDS. These cooperative organizations can be brought under the watchful eyes of the professionals employed under cooperative entrepreneurship development system.

- Production and marketing of cooperative products needs an effective and efficient system of management and administration. Adoption of effective and efficient marketing strategies and practices shall form the centrality of distribution system. New product and development and design can be promoted through cooperative entrepreneurship system. They can obtain knowledge on new products from technical collaboration and cooperation from organizations outside the country. Even inter-cooperative organizational collaboration in new product exchanges can be promoted and developed through cooperative entrepreneurship development system.

- The contribution of cooperative sector in socio economic development is very vital and essential in the 21st century. Therefore, in order to fulfill the socio-economic objectives, the cooperative entrepreneurship development system and its manpower can enter into offering Training and Education on modem management system and technology to various cooperative organizations.

- The ICA, must visualize the need for promoting, cooperative entrepreneurship development system in order to make cooperatives, more relevant in the new centenary. They must identify suitable cooperative sectors and sub-sectors, where cooperative entrepreneurship development system can be more applicable, namely, consumers, health, insurance, tourism, labour, small and medium scale industries, micro enterprises. In all these areas, professionalization and technological skill upgradation and modernization might be essential.

- Bureaucratic instruments and tools and mechanism can be sparingly utilized by the government department. This would reduce multiplicity of controls and administration and even political interference in the bureaucratic set up can be reduced in a phased manner/approach.

- New generation cooperative leadership shall be the sine-qua-non for the prosperity of cooperative entrepreneurship development system. It is the duty and responsibility of enlightened new generation leaders to ensure that cooperative entrepreneurship development system is performing its functions in the most effective and efficient manner.

Conclusion

The bewildering paradox of the global market scenario and economic liberalization has dark and bright side of undertaking several developmental activities in different socio-economic areas in India. By and large the entry of MNC's and LPG's has slowed down the operations of indigenous industries under the umbrella of cooperative manufacturing and industrial institutions. Therefore, there is need for updating and modernizing all cooperative business development activities and even the internal management systems development. The Foreign Direct Investment (FDI) must be allocated into the cooperative sector. They can invest in the training, development and education of cooperative manpower by setting up state of the art Training Institutions, Training Colleges or centers for, cooperative organizations.

The ICA should take suitable and viable steps and provide guidelines in connection with promoting cooperative entrepreneurship system. They can link all the countries having surplus funds which can carry out investment in India. Hiring professionals by cooperative organizations from different progressive organizations and institutions (including, educational (technical) institutions) can form part and parcel of cooperative entrepreneurship system. For better training and development of cooperative entrepreneurs, they must undertake effective and efficient mode of transmitting knowledge and skills. Through this activity the "Brain-Drain from Cooperative Sector to other organizations", can be discouraged and cooperatives can even undertake contracting activities which can be extended to energize cooperative entrepreneurs in the long-run.

References

1. Agya Ram Shakya, (August 2003), Globalization-its consequences on society, third concept, 2003.

2. PA. Mashelker, Indian Innovation Management, NCDC Bulletin, 1999.

3. V. Kulandai Swamy, Cooperative Management; Arudra Academy, Coimbatore.

4. R. Srinivasan, Strategic Management, Prentice Hall of India Private Limited, New Delhi.

5. Reddy, Bheemeshwar, The Status of Public-Agricultural Extension Services: A Case Study in RuralMaharashtra, MA Dissertation in Development Studies, Tata Institute of Social Sciences, Mumbai, 2008.

6. S.D. Sawant, V. Daptardar and S. Mhatre, "Capital Formation and Growth in Agriculture: Neglected Aspects and Dimensions", Economic and Political Weekly, May 16, 2002.

7. Sen and Abhijit "Economic Liberalisation and Agriculture in India", Social Scientist, Vol.20, No.11, Pp. 4-19, 1992.